TELL ME WHY #3

BY ARKADY LEOKUM

ILLUSTRATIONS BY HOWARD BENDER

GROSSET & DUNLAP • New York

Abridged from the original book entitled *Still More Tell Me Why.*

BOMC offers recordings and compact discs, cassettes and records. For information and catalog write to BOMR, Camp Hill, PA 17012.

CONTENTS

Chapter 1
Our World

Chapter 2

How Other Creatures Live

Chapter 3

The Human Body

Chapter 4

How Things Began

Chapter 5

How Things Are Made

TELL ME WHY #3

CHAPTER 1
OUR WORLD

Because in early times the study of plant life dealt mainly with plants as food, it became known as botany, from a Greek word meaning "herb."

The first people to specialize in the study of botany were primitive

WHAT IS BOTANY?

medicine men and witch doctors. They had to know the plants that could kill or cure people. And botany was closely linked with medicine for hundreds of years.

In the sixteenth century, people began to observe plants and write books about their observations. These writers were the "fathers" of modern botany. In the nineteenth century, the work of an English scientist, Charles Darwin, helped botanists gain a better understanding of how plants as well as animals evolved from simpler ancestors. His work led botanists to set up special branches of botany.

One of these branches is "plant anatomy," which has to do with the structure of plants and how they might be related. Experiments on plant heredity were performed to find out how various species came to be and how they could be improved. This study is called "genetics."

"Ecology," another branch of botany, deals with studies of the distribution of plants throughout the world, to find out why certain species grew in certain places. "Paleobotany," another branch, works out plant evolution from the evidence of fossil remains.

Other branches of botany include "plant physiology," which studies the way plants breathe and make food, and "plant pathology," which is concerned with the study of plant diseases.

According to the theories of science, there was a time when there were no plants on earth. Then, hundreds of millions of years ago, tiny specks of protoplasm appeared on the earth. Protoplasm is the name for the living material that is found in both plants and animals. These original specks of protoplasm, according to this theory, were the beginnings of all our plants and animals.

WHERE DO PLANTS COME FROM?

The protoplasm specks that became plants developed thick walls and settled down to staying in one place. They also developed a kind of green coloring matter known as "chlorophyll." This enabled them to make food from substances in the air, water, and soil.

These early green plants had only one cell, but they later formed groups of cells. Since they had no protection against drying out, they had to stay in the water. Today, some descendants of these original plants still survive, though they have changed quite a bit. We call them "algae."

One group of plants developed that obtained its food without the use of chlorophyll. These non-green plants are "the fungi."

Most of the plants on earth today evolved from the algae. Certain of these came out of the sea and developed rootlets that could anchor them in the soil. They also developed little leaves with an outer skin covering as protection against drying. These plants became mosses and ferns.

All of the earliest plants reproduced either by simple cell division or by means of spores. Spores are little dustlike cells something like seeds, but containing no stored food in them as seeds do. As time went on, some of these plants developed flowers that produced true seeds.

Two different types of plants with seeds appeared. Those with naked seeds and those with protected seeds. Each of these two types later developed along many different lines.

If you were to cut down any tree more than one year old and look at the cross section, you would see alternating bands of light and dark wood. The two bands together are called "the annual ring," and they make up the amount of wood formed by the tree during a single growing season or year.

WHAT MAKES THE RINGS ON A TREE?

Why are the bands lighter and darker? This is because the wood grows in a different way during the different seasons. In spring and early summer, the cells of the wood are bigger and have thinner walls. This makes them look lighter. In late summer, the cells are smaller, have thick walls, and are closely packed together. This makes a darker band.

The age of a tree can be told by counting the annual rings. When you look at the rings of a tree, you will notice that they vary in width and in many other details. These variations are caused by the weather conditions that prevailed during the given season. A difference in the light, the amount of rain, and the minerals in the soil, will produce a difference in the rings of a tree. That is why scientists often use the rings to obtain a clue to the weather conditions that prevailed years ago in certain parts of the world.

When a tree grows, the wood of the tree is not the only thing that increases in size from year to year. Additions are also made to the bark of the tree. This is done by means of a thin band of living, dividing cells between the wood and the bark. This layer is called "the cambium." The new cells which are formed on the wood side of the cambium become wood. The cells formed toward the outside become bark.

The outer portion of a woody stem or root is called "bark." Sometimes it is hard to tell how much of the stem should be called bark. In the palm tree, for example, there is no clear separation between bark and wood.

WHY DO TREES HAVE BARK?

What does bark do for the tree? One of its main functions is to protect the inner, more delicate structures. It not only keeps them from drying out, but also guards against outside injuries of various sorts.

The thick, fibrous barks of some redwood trees show burns and scars as a result of fires near the ground, but the inner portions of the tree escaped injury.

The process by which bark is formed may go on year after year. In the very young branch of a maple, for example, there is at first no rough bark. The surface of the shoot is nearly smooth. As the twig forms more wood and grows in size, the outer portions may split open. The injury caused in this way is healed from the inside.

Some of the outer portions become dry and die. The dead, broken portions give the bark a rough appearance. Some of the dry pieces are shed or broken off as the twig grows larger and older.

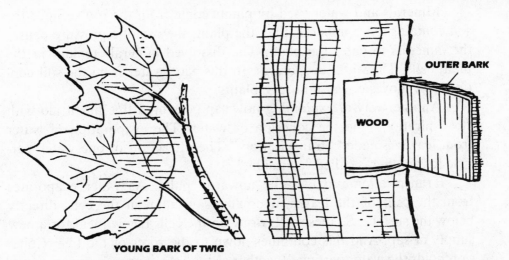

YOUNG BARK OF TWIG

OUTER BARK

WOOD

Man finds the bark of many trees very useful. Commercial cork is obtained almost entirely from the cork oak tree. The bark of the hemlock tree is used in the tanning of leather. The spice we know as cinnamon is the powdered bark of a tree which grows in India and Malaya. Quinine is obtained from the bark of the cinchona tree. Extracts from the bark of other trees are used for flavoring, and the bark of the roots and branches of many trees are used in medicines.

Every single part of the human body receives a constant supply of blood which is pumped by the heart. In plants and trees, every single part receives water and nourishment, which we call sap. But a tree has no pump because it has no heart. Then how does the sap go up a tree?

WHAT MAKES SAP GO UP A TREE?

Science still cannot explain this mystery exactly! Of course there are several theories about it, but no single theory seems to offer the complete answer. Scientists believe that there are several forces at work to make this possible.

One explanation has to do with "osmotic pressure." In living things, liquids and dissolved materials pass through membranes. This is called "osmosis." When there are dissolved chemicals in contact with a membrane, they press against the membrane. This is called "osmotic pressure." If there are many particles in a solution, more particles press against the membrane and seep through than in solutions with fewer particles.

Minerals and water used by plants come from the roots. Since the soil contains more minerals than the plant, the osmotic pressure causes the minerals to enter the plant. The dissolved minerals remain in the plant cells. The water evaporates. In this way, water from the soil continuously moves upward through plants.

Another way of explaining how sap goes up a tree has to do with "transpiration" and the cohesion of water. The evaporation of water from leaves is called "transpiration." The attraction of one water particle for another is called "cohesion."

Transpiration provides the upward "pull." As water evaporates from the cells of the leaves, it creates a vacuum in the cells directly below the surface. So these cells draw on the cells below them for a new supply of sap. And this continues down to the roots of the tree Cohesion holds the water particles together as they move up.

We know that human beings and animals have to find ways to protect themselves against enemies. Plants need protection to survive too. One of the natural protections a plant can have is a poison which makes it dangerous to eat or even touch the plant.

WHAT IS POISON IVY?

One of the most common poisonous plants in North America is poison ivy. Contact with this plant causes an inflammation and itching, though not everyone is affected by it in the same way.

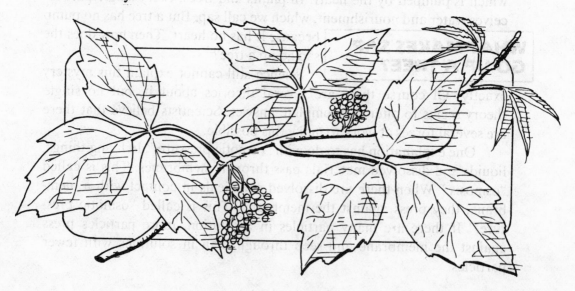

Poison ivy grows in the United States as far west as eastern Texas, eastern Kansas, and Minnesota. It climbs up the tall trunks of trees, grows among bushes along the road, and may even grow in sandy places where most other plants cannot grow.

Usually it is a three-leafed vine, but sometimes it grows in an upright, shrubby way. It stays shining green even in the driest hot days of summer. In the autumn it changes to rich shades of scarlet.

The poison that is in poison ivy is an oil called "toxicodendrol." It is found in all parts of the plant, not just the leaves. This is why cases of poison ivy can develop at all seasons of the year.

About one person in five is not subject to ivy poisoning in any way. Many people believe when the fluid in the blisters which form is spread on other parts of the body, the poisoning will spread. But this is not so. What happens is that the effects of the poisoning appear on various parts of the body to begin with.

There are enough varieties of apples to satisfy everybody's taste. In the United States alone, more than 7,000 varieties of apples have been recorded. And when you consider the whole world, there are probably a few thousand more.

HOW MANY KINDS OF APPLES ARE THERE?

We know that it is one of the earliest fruits raised by man. The apple probably originated in southeastern Europe and southwestern Asia, and was eaten and raised by the very earliest inhabitants there. More than 2,000 years ago, different varieties of apples were already being raised in Europe. In ancient Rome, the natives enjoyed seven different varieties of apples.

How are all these varieties obtained? A great deal of experimenting is always being carried on by apple growers. When you graft a bud or twig of any given variety onto any kind of young apple tree, the mature tree yields apples of the same variety as the graft. So nurserymen always experiment with grafting and by fertilizing the blossoms to cross-breed them.

Sometimes a new variety appears unexpectedly. The Red Delicious appeared in this way. An ordinary tree, producing average good fruit, grew one branch on which appeared apples quite different from the rest. A new variety of apple was born!

Not so long ago in West Virginia, there were some gnarled old apple trees that yielded only a small, bitter, misshapen fruit. The farmer, a patient man, experimented with seedlings for a long time. Then finally one autumn he received his reward. From one of the young trees hung a heavy crop of luscious fruit, now known as Golden Delicious.

The banyan tree is one of the giants among trees. Anything in nature that is a "giant" presents all kinds of problems, and trees are no exception.

For example, a giant tree has the problem of drawing water from the

WHAT IS A BANYAN TREE?

roots to the top. The trunk of the tree must be strong. A tree cannot grow too tall and remain slender, or it would break. So a giant tree must be wider at the base to support the load above it. And if the branches are large and heavy, they could pull down the trunk to one side or another.

The banyan tree is a giant tree that has solved these problems in an interesting way. It is a tree of the mulberry family, and it is found in eastern India and near Malaysia.

The most unusual thing about the banyan tree is the way its branches grow. They spread out in all directions all around the trunk. And even though the trunk is huge, it cannot support these branches. So thick roots grow from the underside of the branches directly to the ground.

When these roots take hold, they provide support and nourishment for the tree. They also develop into new trunks. The result is that the ban-

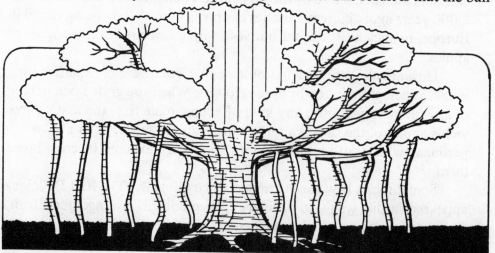

yan tree grows more in circumference than in height. Eventually, "arcades" of these roots are formed, and a banyan tree may have a circumference that reaches 1,500 feet!

These arcades of roots are actually used as marketplaces by people, who find it a perfect sheltered place to gather and do business. If these roots are cut, they are useful for making tent poles and the fiber is used for making rope.

The banyan tree produces tiny figs. When they become ripe they are bright red and are eaten by birds and bats.

The flower is the means by which the plant can reproduce new plants like itself. A botanist defines a flower as a group of parts whose function is to produce pollen or seeds or both.

WHAT IS POLLINATION?

The most important parts of the flower, from this point of view, are "pistils" and "stamens." Many flowers contain both, the pistil or pistils in the center, surrounded by the stamens.

In the enlarged, bottom part of the pistil there are tiny bodies called "ovules." Each ovule may develop into a seed. The most important part of an ovule is a tiny egg cell, so small it can only be seen under a microscope.

The stamens contain a pollen sac at the end of a stalk. When these pollen sacs open, they release the pollen they contain as a fine dust which is usually yellow.

In order to produce new seeds, the pollen grains from the stamens must be transferred to the pistils. This transfer of pollen is called "pollination."

Pollination is brought about in many different ways. Sometimes the pollen simply falls onto the pistil, but usually the wind or insects are needed for pollination.

Among the plants that are pollinated by the wind are the grasses; not just the grasses of the meadows, but wheat, corn, and other grains. The stamens wave in the breeze. The pollen is shaken off and flies through the air and lands on pistils.

Another form of pollination is carried on by insects. This usually happens with flowers that have bright colors or fragrance, and thus attract insects. Insects visit the flower for nectar which they make into honey, and for pollen which they use as food. As an insect collects pollen from a flower, some of it rubs off on the insect's body. Then when the insect visits another flower, some of the pollen rubs onto the stamens.

Sometimes toadstools seem to appear as if by magic on a lawn after a rainy day. But of course no magic is involved. Toadstools grow from spores. And toadstools and mushrooms are exactly the same thing. There is no difference between them.

WHERE DO TOADSTOOLS COME FROM?

A typical mushroom consists of a cylindrical stem, or "stipe," supporting a circular cap, or "pileus." On the stipe is a collar known as a ring, or "annulus." Radiating from the stipe to the margin of the cap on its underside are gills, or "lamellae." This is where the spores are formed.

Spores have a similar purpose to that of seeds, but they should not be confused with seeds. Spores are produced in great quantities. In fact, so many are produced by a mushroom, that there is a good chance the wind will carry some of them to spots favorable for growth.

If a spore falls in a place that is warm and moist and where food is available, the spore, which consists of a single cell, begins to absorb nourishment. It grows by division until long chains of cells resembling threads are formed. Such a chain is called a "hypha." A tangle of them is called a "mycelium." At various points along the mycelium, tiny balls no bigger than pinheads develop and become mushrooms.

So you see that when mushrooms or toadstools seem to appear suddenly, it is really the end of a long process that started with the spores leaving some mushroom that could have been quite a distance away!

"Force" is a push or a pull which changes the motion, or movement, of objects. When you push a chair, you are exerting force on it. When you stop pushing, the chair stops moving. But suppose you roll a ball along the ground. It keeps on rolling after you have stopped pushing it! Why?

WHAT IS CENTRIFUGAL FORCE?

The explanation for this (developed by Sir Isaac Newton, the first scientist to explain the theories of force) is the idea of "inertia." Inertia makes an object keep up whatever motion it has. Every bit of matter has inertia and will keep moving in a straight line at the same speed unless another force changes its motion. For example, if you are riding in a bus and the driver jams on the brakes, your body will hurl forward because of its inertia—it will keep on going forward at the same speed the bus was traveling.

Now let us get to centrifugal force. All of us have experienced this force. We notice it whenever an object travels in a curved path. Let us say you are on that same bus and it suddenly turns a corner. You will probably find yourself falling off the seat into the aisle! The reason is centrifugal force.

Centrifugal force can be explained by using the idea of inertia. When the bus turns, inertia tends to keep your body moving in a straight line. So you tend to move toward the outside of the curve so as to keep your original straight motion. Centrifugal force always seems to push objects to the outside of the curve.

This is why highways are often tilted around a turn; why airplanes bank when they turn; and why, when you are riding a bicycle, you lean inward! This leaning inward, and the banking of roads and airplanes, helps to balance centrifugal force, which would otherwise tend to hurl objects outward. The leaning inward balances the tendency to move outward and you can make the turn properly.

We speak of ordinary light as being "white"; we call it white light, or sunlight. But this light is really a mixture of all colors.

When sunlight strikes the beveled edge of a mirror, or the edge of a

glass prism, or the surface of a soap bubble, we see the colors in light. What happens is that the white light is broken up into the different wave lengths that are seen by our eyes as red, orange, yellow, green, blue, and violet.

These wave lengths form a band of parallel stripes, each color grading into the one next to it. This band is called a "spectrum." In the spectrum, the red line is always at one end and the blue and violet lines at the other end, and this is decided by their different wave lengths.

When we see a rainbow, it is just as if we were looking at such a spectrum. In fact, a rainbow is simply a great curve spectrum caused by the breaking up of sunlight.

When sunlight enters a droplet of water, it is broken up just as if it had entered a glass prism. So inside the drop of water, we already have the different colors going from one side of the drop to the other. Some of this colored light is then reflected from the far side of the droplet, back and out of the droplet.

The light comes back out of the droplet in different directions, depending on the color. And when you look at these colors in a rainbow, you see them arranged with red at the top and violet at the bottom of the rainbow.

A rainbow is seen only during showers when rain is falling and the sun shining at the same time, but on opposite sides of the observer. You have to be between the sun and the droplets of water with the sun at your back. The sun, your eye, and the center of the arc of the rainbow must all be in a straight line.

One of the great mysteries of the world in which we live is light. We still do not know exactly what it is. It can be described only in terms of what it does.

HOW DOES LIGHT TRAVEL?

We know light is a form of energy. Like some other forms of energy—heat, radio waves, and X-rays—the speed, frequency, and length of its waves can be measured. Its behavior in other ways makes it similar to these other forms of energy, too.

We know the speed of light. It travels at about 186,000 miles per second. This means that in a year, a beam of light travels 5,880,000,000,000 miles. That is the distance which astronomers call a "light year," and it is the unit used to measure distances in outer space.

In trying to understand what light was and how it traveled, many theories have been developed. In the seventeenth century, Sir Isaac Newton said that light must be made up of "corpuscles," somewhat like tiny bullets shot from the light source. But this "corpuscular" theory of light could not explain many of the ways in which light behaved.

At about the same time, a man named Christian Huygens developed a "wave theory" of light. His idea was that a luminous or lighted particle started pulses, or waves, much as a pebble dropped into a pool makes waves.

Whether light was waves or corpuscles was argued for nearly 150 years. Gradually, as certain effects of light became known, the idea of light corpuscles died out.

Scientists now believe that light behaves both as particles and as waves. Experiments can show either idea to be true. So we simply cannot give a complete answer to "What is light?"

A molecule is the smallest bit of a substance that can exist and still keep the properties of the whole. For example, if you broke down a molecule of sugar, the elements would not have the characteristics of sugar—its taste or its color, among other things.

HOW BIG IS A MOLECULE?

Some molecules are very simple, others have thousands of atoms arranged in a complicated pattern. In some gases, such as helium and neon, a molecule consists of only one atom. Some molecules contain two or more atoms of the same kind. A molecule of water, for example, is made up of two atoms of hydrogen and one of oxygen.

In contrast, the molecule of pure natural rubber is thought to contain about 75,000 carbon atoms and about 120,000 hydrogen atoms. So you can see that molecules differ greatly in size.

Simple molecules like that of water are only a few billionths of an inch in length. The rubber molecule is thousands of times larger. Some molecules are shaped like footballs, others are long and threadlike.

It is really impossible for us to imagine how small molecules are. For example, let us take a single cubic inch of air. In this space there are 500 billion billion molecules (5 with 20 zeroes after it). And that cubic inch of air is not packed tightly because it actually contains a great deal of empty space.

The weight of a molecule is measured by scientists on a relative scale. The weight of the molecule depends upon the weight of the atoms that form it. And the weight of the atom, in turn, depends upon the number of protons and neutrons in the nucleus of the atom.

DOES A MOLECULE HAVE WEIGHT?

A molecule of water is made up of two atoms of hydrogen plus one of oxygen. Hydrogen is a simple atom with only one proton in the nucleus. Its atomic weight is 1. The weight of other elements is in multiples of the weight of hydrogen. Oxygen has eight protons and eight neutrons, making an atomic weight of 16. So, water has a molecular weight of 2 x 1 plus 16, which makes its molecular weight 18.

Molecules are held in their places in a solid or a liquid by the forces of attraction between molecules. This attraction is of an electrical nature, and this force is strong enough to account for the strength of most solid materials.

All material things on earth are made up of one or more elements. Elements are substances that have atoms of only one kind.

Any one element may have some of the same properties that other

WHAT ARE THE ELEMENTS?

elements have, but no two elements are exactly alike. For example, hydrogen and helium are both colorless, odorless, and tasteless gases. They are both light, but helium is heavier. Hydrogen burns, but helium will not.

All elements have a certain weight. They can be a solid, a liquid, or a gas. Some will dissolve in water. Others must be heated to a certain temperature before they will change from a solid to a liquid or to a gas. These characteristics are called "the physical properties" of elements.

After scientists studied the physical and chemical properties of elements, they grouped the elements that were alike together. These elements are called "chemical families."

All the families were combined into "the periodic table of elements." They were listed in order of their "atomic number." The atomic number of an element depends on how many protons, particles with a positive charge, the atom of each element contains. A hydrogen atom has one proton and its atomic number is one, so it is first on the periodic table.

Some elements are named after people or places or countries: Einsteinium, Europium, Germanium, Californium, and Scandium. Among the familiar elements are carbon, copper, gold, iron, lead, mercury, nickel, platinum, tin, radium, and silver.

People have been terrified of quicksand for centuries. It is supposed to have the mysterious power of sucking victims into it until they disappear.

The truth is, quicksand has no such power. And the fact is that if you

WHAT IS QUICKSAND?

know what it is and how to deal with it, it cannot hurt you at all.

What is quicksand? It is a light, loose sand which is mixed with water. It does not look different from sands which might be right next to it. But there is a difference: quicksand will not support heavy objects.

Quicksand usually occurs near the mouths of large rivers and on flat shores where there is a layer of stiff clay under it. Water is collected in the sand because the underlying clay keeps the water from draining away. This water may come from many different places, such as river currents or pools.

The grains of quicksand are different from ordinary grains of sand because they are round instead of being angular or sharp. The water gets between the grains and separates and lifts them, so that they tend to flow over one another. This makes them unable to support solid objects.

Some quicksand is not even made of sand. It can be any kind of loose soil, a mixture of sand and mud, or a kind of pebbly mud.

People who step into quicksand do not sink out of sight. Since it contains so much liquid, it will enable them to float. And since quicksand is heavier than water, people can float higher in it than they do in water.

The important thing is to move slowly in quicksand. This is to give it time to flow around the body. Once it does this, it will act like water in which you are swimming.

The dust and other materials that are in the air as the result of a nuclear explosion—that is, from atom bombs—is fallout. It contaminates, or poisons, the air, soil, and water.

WHAT IS FALLOUT?

Fallout contaminates the world around us because it is radioactive. This means that it contains certain kinds of atoms that are breaking down. As they break down, they give off tiny amounts of energy and matter, which are called "radiations."

A nuclear explosion produces a huge blast, a lot of heat, and many radioactive atoms. These radioactive atoms become mixed with particles of soil and dust from the earth. Tons of radioactive dust are blown or sucked into the atmosphere by a nuclear explosion. This returns to earth as radioactive fallout.

The heaviest particles of this debris drops to earth within minutes or a few hours after a nuclear explosion. The lighter particles are carried up and come down more slowly. They may circle the earth for months or even years. Eventually, they fall to the earth, mostly in snow, rain, and mist.

Fallout that falls on the outside of the human body can be washed away. But if fallout radiation gets inside the body, it may stay there for years. Fallout enters the body with the air, water, and food taken in. Mainly it comes from food. Fallout dusts the leaves of plants and their fruits. It falls on the soil and is taken into plants through their roots. Animals eat the plants, then human beings and other animals eat these animals.

Inside the body, radioactive atoms from the fallout send off radiations. When too much radiation passes through living cells, it may damage the cells or weaken the body's defenses against disease.

Platinum is a metal—but what an amazing metal it is! It is grayish white in color, and its names comes from the Spanish *plata* and means "little silver."

WHAT IS PLATINUM?

Platinum is harder than copper and almost as pliable as gold. You could take a single ounce of platinum and stretch it out into a fine wire that would reach from New York City to New Orleans, Louisiana. A cube of platinum measuring a foot each way would have a weight of more than half a ton! Platinum is almost twice as heavy as lead.

Platinum is usually found in ores often mixed with the rare metals palladium, rhodium, iridium, and osmium, which are called "platinum metals." Occasionally, it is found with metals such as gold, copper, silver, iron, chromium, and nickel. It is found in the form of small grains, scales, or nuggets.

Large deposits of platinum were first discovered in South America in the eighteenth century. For a great many years it was considered quite useless, and so it was cheap. Then, when people began to find how useful this metal could be, and since it is quite rare, the price went up to the point where that cube of platinum mentioned above would have been worth $2,500,000.

What makes platinum especially useful is that it resists oxidation, acids, and heat. The melting point of platinum is about 3,190 degrees Fahrenheit! For most purposes, platinum is mixed (alloyed) with one of the other "platinum metals" or with silver, gold, copper, nickel, or tin.

While the chief use of platinum is for jewelry, it is also used for contact points where electrical circuits are opened or closed, in laboratory weights, in instruments for exact measurement of temperatures, and for fuses in delicate electric instruments.

Many people consider milk to be the most nearly perfect food we have. And when you consider all the good things for your body that you obtain when you drink milk, you can see why this is so.

WHAT IS MILK MADE OF?

Proteins used to build and repair muscles are found in milk. Another important part of milk is fat, an energy-giving food. The fat in milk is called "butterfat." When globules (tiny, round pieces of fat) are present in milk, butter can be made.

Milk also has sugar, which is an energy-giving carbohydrate. Lactose, the sugar found in milk, is less sweet than cane sugar, and is more easily used by the body than is any other kind of sugar.

Milk also supplies the body with important minerals. The body uses minerals as bone-building and blood-building foods. Calcium and phosphorous make up a large part of the mineral content of milk. There is more calcium in milk than in any other food.

Other minerals in milk are iron, copper, manganese, magnesium, sodium, potassium, chlorine, iodine, cobalt, and zinc. And we're not finished yet! Milk also provides us with many vitamins. Milk is rich in vitamins B_2, A, B_1. It also contains vitamins C and D. And, of course, milk also contains water. But the amazing thing is that there is about a quarter of a pound of food solids in each quart of milk!

Early man, living thousands of years ago, made caves and rock shelters his home. In fact, some of the earliest cave dwellers did not even look like people living today.

WHO WERE THE CAVE MEN?

These were the Neanderthal people. Their brains were as large as modern man's, but they had rugged faces with heavy ridges over their eyes. They were only a little over five feet in height and could not stand as straight as people do today.

These "cave men" or cave dwellers, were not good housekeepers. Anything they did not want, they left on the floor of the cave. Over thousands of years this mass of rubbish piled up and sometimes filled the caves.

The caves were large, dark, and frightening. The people lived in the mouth of the cave where they were protected from wind, rain, and snow, without going into the darkness deep in the cave.

During the last part of the Ice Age, Cro-Magnon men, people who looked much like people living today, started to move into Europe. Like the Neanderthals before them, they lived in the mouths of caves.

But there were not enough caves for everyone, so some made tents and underground houses to live in. These are the men who made the famous cave paintings found in southern France and northwestern Spain.

These paintings are quite remarkable. They are full of life and power, and show many of the animals these cave dwellers hunted, such as the bison, the bear, the wild boar, the mammoth, and the rhinoceros.

Far back in prehistory, before man could write, was a period of time known as the Stone Age. Man has lived on the earth for at least 500,000 years, but he did not begin to write until about 5,000 years ago. So prehistory covers a very long time.

WHAT WAS THE STONE AGE?

Because man learned to make stone tools during this time, it is called the Stone Age. The early part of it is known as the Old Stone Age.

The first type of stone tool that was made was probably a big stone chipped so that it had a sharp cutting edge all around. Scientists have called it a "hard ax." Chips struck off pieces of stone were also used as tools. The hand ax and the chips, or flakes, were all-purpose tools that man kept making and using for thousands of years.

Later, in the Ice Age, there were people living in Europe who are called Neanderthal by scientists. They had better tools than the people who had lived in the earliest days, and they hunted in groups instead of alone.

After the Neanderthals came the Cro-Magnon men, who were a more advanced people. They had all kinds of tools: spear points, harpoons, scrapers, and knives. They too lived by hunting.

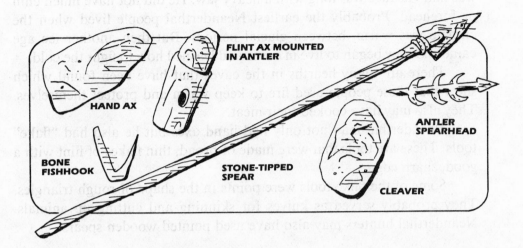

HAND AX

FLINT AX MOUNTED IN ANTLER

ANTLER SPEARHEAD

BONE FISHHOOK

STONE-TIPPED SPEAR

CLEAVER

About 6000 B.C., there came a great change in man's way of life. He learned to grow crops. This marked the beginning of the Neolithic, or New Stone Age.

He used animals as a source for food and the skins for clothing. He kept flocks of animals, built homes, and soon began to make new things that were not found in nature.

Clay could be molded into dishes and bowls. When it was baked it could be used for cooking food. Wool and flax could be spun into yarn. When men worked together, villages and then cities grew. And from these beginnings all that we call civilization came into being.

In trying to learn how man developed, scientists study whatever remains of prehistoric man they can find. These include tools, cooking utensils, skeletons, and parts of the body.

WHO WAS NEANDERTHAL MAN?

In 1856, the remains of men were dug from a limestone cave in the Neander Gorge in Germany. These were the first complete skeletons ever found of prehistoric men, and this was because these people buried their dead.

Neanderthal people probably lived for about 70,000 years in central Asia, the Middle East, and many parts of Europe. This was in a period of about 150,000 to 30,000 years ago.

What was Neanderthal man like? He was heavy and stocky. His skull was flat. His face was long with a heavy jaw. He did not have much chin or forehead. Probably the earliest Neanderthal people lived when the climate was warm, between glacial periods. But then another ice age came and they began to live in caves and learned how to fight the cold.

There are many hearths in the caves that have been found which show that these people used fire to keep warm and protect themselves. They also may have cooked their meat.

Neanderthal man not only had hand axes but he also had "flake" tools. These are tools that were made of broad, thin flakes of flint with a good, sharp edge.

Some of the flake tools were points in the shape of rough triangles. They probably served as knives for skinning and cutting up animals. Neanderthal hunters may also have used pointed wooden spears.

Deserts have come to symbolize for us places of extreme heat. The fact is, most of the famous deserts of the world are places where the thermometer goes bubbling away and where the sun beats down without mercy.

ARE DESERTS ALWAYS HOT?

But this does not mean that a desert must be a place where it is always hot! Let us get a definition of a desert and we will see why this is so. A desert is a region where only special forms of life can exist because there is a shortage of moisture.

In a "hot" desert, there simply is not enough rainfall. So the definition holds true. But suppose there is a region where all water is frozen solid and cannot be used by plants. This satisfies the definition too. Only it would make this a "cold" desert!

Did you know, for example, that much of the Arctic is really a desert? There is less than 15 inches of rainfall a year, and most of the water is frozen. So it is quite properly called a desert. The great Gobi Desert in the middle of Asia is bitterly cold in winter time!

Most of the dry, hot deserts with which we are familiar are found in two belts around the world, just north and south of the Equator. They are caused by high atmospheric pressures that exist in those areas and prevent rain from falling. Other deserts, which are found farther away from the Equator, are the result of being in "the rain shadow." This is the name for an effect that is caused by mountain barriers that catch rainfall on their seaward side and leave the interior region dry.

No great rivers originate in deserts. But a river may rise in moister areas and cross great deserts on their way to the sea. The Nile, for example, flows through the desert region of the Sahara and the Colorado River flows through a desert too.

If you lived near a coast line, or have ever visited the coast, then you have probably seen the great difference that can exist between high tide and low tide. Boats that float in the water at high tide may be sitting on

dry land at low tide, and a big area of beach or land be exposed. In some parts of the world, the height of high tide above low is more than 40 feet!

Obviously, this movement of water is a great source of unused energy. If this energy could be put to work, as it is from waterfalls and rivers, the power would be enormous. For example, if a large bay could be dammed so that it did not empty at low tide, the water could then be turned into electric power by directing it through power plants.

But so far this has been only on a small scale. The ocean tides can be useful to man, but he simply has not been willing, or has not found it necessary, to spend the money and do the work to use this energy.

The outside of the earth is a crust of rock which is about 10 to 30 miles thick. When we go down into this crust, we find that it begins to get hotter and hotter.

WHY IS IT HOT INSIDE THE EARTH?

For about every 60 feet we go down, the temperature grows one degree higher. At two miles below the surface of the earth, the temperature is high enough to boil water! If it were possible to dig down 30 miles, the temperature would be about 2,200 degrees Fahrenheit. This is hot enough to melt rocks. At the center of the earth, scientists believe the temperature to be about 10,000 degrees Fahrenheit.

The crust of the earth has two layers. The upper layer, which makes the continents, is made up of granite. Under the layer of granite is a thick layer of very hard black rock called "basalt." This layer supports the continents and forms the basins that hold the oceans. At the center of the earth, it is believed that there is a huge ball of molten iron, with a diameter of about 4,000 miles.

How did the center of the earth get to be this way? According to most scientific theories, the earth and sun were once related in some way. Most scientists believe that the earth was once a hot, whirling mass of gas, liquid, or solid that began its regular trips around the sun. As years went by, it slowly cooled and the large mass grew smaller. As it whirled, it slowly took a ball-like shape. It was red-hot and held in its path by the attraction of the sun.

As the earth cooled, a hard crust formed on the surface. Nobody knows how long it took for the crust to form. But underneath that crust there remained the hot center core of the earth, and it is still there today.

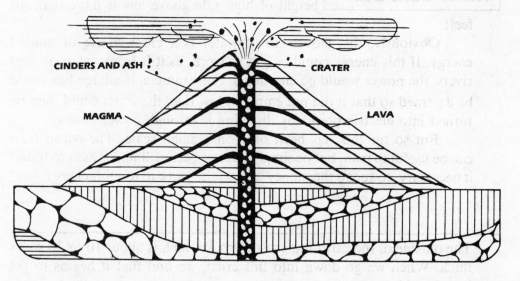

In February, 1943, in the middle of a cornfield in Mexico, people saw a rare and amazing thing taking place. A volcano was being born! In three months it had formed a cone about 1,000 feet high. Two towns were destroyed and a wide area damaged by the falling ash and cinders.

HOW DOES A VOLCANO FORM?

What makes a volcano form? The temperature under the surface of the earth becomes higher and higher the deeper you go down. At a depth of about 20 miles, it is hot enough to melt most rocks.

When rock melts, it expands and needs more space. In certain areas of the world, mountains are being uplifted. The pressure becomes less under these rising mountain ranges, and a reservoir of melted rock (called "magma") may form under them.

This material rises along cracks formed by the uplift. When the pressure in the reservoir is greater than the roof of rock over it, it bursts forth as a volcano.

In the eruption, hot gaseous, liquid, or solid material is blown out. The material piles up around the opening, and a cone-shaped mound is formed. The "crater" is the depression at the top of the cone where the opening reaches the surface. The cone is the result of a volcano.

The material coming out of a volcano is mainly gaseous, but large quantities of "lava" and solid particles that look like cinders and ash are also thrown out.

Actually, lava is magma that has been thrown up by the volcano. When the magma comes near the surface, the temperature and the pressure drop, and a physical and chemical change takes place that changes the magma to lava.

You can get a pretty good idea of what causes an earthquake from thinking about what happens during an earthquake. During an earthquake, there is a trembling of the ground. It is this trembling of the earth which may cause buildings to fall.

HOW DOES AN EARTHQUAKE START?

So an earthquake is a trembling or vibration of the earth's surface. What makes it happen? Well, the rock of the earth's crust may have a "fault," a kind of break in the crust. The earth blocks shift. Sometimes the sides of the fault move up and down against each other. At other times, the sides of the fault shift lengthwise.

But when one rock mass has rubbed on another with great force and friction, we have a lot of energy being used. This vast energy that comes from the rubbing is changed to vibration in the rocks. The vibration is what we feel as an earthquake. And this vibration may travel thousands of miles.

The reason earthquakes take place in certain regions frequently and almost never in other regions, is that the faults in the earth's crust are located in these regions.

There are many things about our own earth that still remain a mystery to us, and one of them is how the oceans were formed.

Actually, we do not even know for sure how old the oceans are.

HOW WERE THE OCEANS FORMED?

It seems certain that oceans did not exist in the first stage of the earth's growth. Perhaps they first came into being as clouds of vapor which turned into water as the earth grew cool. Estimates have been made of the ocean's age based on the amount of mineral salt in the ocean today. These estimates range between 500,000,000 and 1,000,000,000 years.

Scientists are pretty sure that most of the earth's land was covered by the sea at one time in the past. Some areas of the earth have been under water several times. But we do not know if any part of the deep ocean ever was land, or whether any land existing today was once beneath the deep ocean.

There is a great deal of evidence to show that certain parts of the land were once the bottom of shallow seas. For example, most of the limestone, sandstone, and shale found on land were deposited as sediment. The chalk that is found in England, Texas, and Kansas was deposited on the bed of a sea. It is made up of the shells of tiny creatures that sank to the ocean bed to form what we call chalk.

Today, the waters of all the oceans cover nearly three-quarters of the surface of the earth. While there are many great ocean areas where man has not yet explored the bottom or taken soundings, we have a good, rough idea of what the bottom is like. There are sections that are like mountain ranges, and there are plateaus and plains. But the ocean bottom is not as varied as the surface of the continents.

Rain and other water on the earth's surface is constantly being carried off. Rivers are the larger streams that accomplish this task. Streams smaller than rivers are brooks. And still smaller streams are rivulets.

HOW DO RIVERS FORM?

These flow together and join until the growing stream may become a large river.

Many rivers flow into the sea. But some rivers flow into inland lakes, and rivers that enter dry plains may even grow smaller and smaller until they disappear by evaporation or by sinking into the dry soil.

River water comes in part from rain water that flows along the ground into the stream channel. Or the river water may come from melting snow and ice, from springs, and from lakes.

Large rivers have many tributaries, or smaller streams, that flow into the main stream. The Ohio and Missouri—which are giant rivers themselves—are really tributaries of the still greater Mississippi. Each tributary has its own smaller tributaries, so that a great river system like the Mississippi is composed of thousands of rivers, creeks, brooks, and rivulets.

The land drained by a river system is called its "drainage basin," or "watershed." The Missouri-Mississippi, which is about 3,890 miles long, drains about 1,243,700 square miles. The Amazon River, some 3,900 miles long, has a watershed of over 2,722,000 square miles!

Rivers wear away the land and carry it, bit by bit, into the sea. During thousands of years, this can cause great erosion in the land. The Grand Canyon and the Delaware Water Gap show how rivers can cut great valleys into the land.

Meteors, also called "shooting stars," have long been a mystery to man.

Today, astronomers feel they have a pretty good idea of what meteors are. They believe them to be broken fragments of comets. When

WHAT ARE METEORS MADE OF?

comets break up, the millions of fragments continue to move through space as a meteor swarm or stream. The swarms move in regular orbits, or paths, through space. Some of the larger fragments may become detached and travel through space singly.

Most individual meteors are quite small, but occasionally there are some that weigh many tons. They are usually destroyed entirely by heat when they pass through the earth's atmosphere. Only the larger ones reach the earth.

When a piece of meteor reaches the earth it is called a "meteorite." The largest one found so far weighs between 60 and 70 tons and is still in its resting place in Africa.

There are two main kinds of meteorites. There are those composed chiefly of nickel and iron. These are called the "metallic" meteorites. Some are composed of minerals and look like a piece of igneous rock (rock formed by intense heat). These are called the "stony" meteorites or "aerolites." The outer surfaces of either kind usually have black crusts which are the result of the terrific heat experienced in passing through the atmosphere to earth.

A star is a ball of very hot gas which shines by its own light. Planets, as you know, and our moon too, shine only by light reflected from the sun. And planets shine with a steady light while stars appear to twinkle. This

is caused by substances in the air between the star and the earth. The unsteady air bends the light from the star, and then it seems to twinkle.

Why does our sun shine? Because it is a star! And not a very big or bright star at that. Compared to all the other stars in the sky, it might be considered medium-sized and medium-bright. There are millions of stars that are smaller than our sun. And many stars are several hundred times larger than the sun. They look small only because they are so far away.

Ever since the days of the Greek astronomers, some 2,000 years ago, the stars have been divided into classes according to their "magnitude," or brightness. Another way of grouping stars is according to their spectra, or the kind of light that comes from the stars. By studying the differences in these spectra, the astronomer may learn about the colors, the temperature, and even the chemical composition of the stars!

You've heard the expression: "As sure as the sun will rise tomorrow." The sun is for us a pretty steady and dependable thing. Whether we see it or not, we know it is always there, shining in the same old way.

DOES THE SUN SHINE THE SAME ALL THE TIME?

And for all practical purposes, that is good enough. The sun is a star, and so it shines by its own light. Where does it get this energy? It is now believed that hydrogen atoms in the very hot interior of the sun combine to form helium. When this happens, it sets free energy which flows steadily to its surface. And the sun should be able to continue radiating this energy for many billions of years to come.

But if we examine the sun in a little more detail, we do not get quite the same "steady" picture. First of all, the sun is not a solid body like the earth, at least at its surface. In fact, different parts of the sun rotate at different rates. The sun's rate of rotation increases from 25 days at its equator to 34 days at its poles.

The outer layer of the sun, called "the corona," is composed of light, gaseous matter. The outer part of this corona is white, and it has streamers that extend out millions of miles from the edge of the sun. These may cause small, but definite differences in the way the sun shines.

Another layer of the sun, called "the chromosphere," is about 9,000 miles thick and is made up largely of hydrogen and helium gas. From this there project huge clouds called "prominences," which may rise to heights of 1,000,000 miles. These also are part of the "unsteady" way the sun shines.

Without the sun, life would be impossible on earth. Among other things, the atmosphere would be frozen, no green plants would be living, and there would be no rain. So we think of the sun as some kind of very special thing in the sky.

WHAT IS THE ORIGIN OF THE SUN?

But there is really nothing special about the sun. It is just a star! Not the biggest or the smallest, not the brightest or the dullest—just an ordinary star like billions of others in the universe! It happens to be the nearest star to us, and we are at just the distance from it that makes it possible to enjoy the benefits of its heat and energy.

Since the sun is a star, scientists cannot really know what its origin was—because they still do not know how the stars in the universe came to be. In fact, there are many things about the sun that cannot be explained. What keeps it "burning," for instance? Well, the sun does not really "burn." It is believed that heat and pressure in the sun change matter into energy. So the sun is using up its matter to send out all that energy.

But this energy is produced at such a great rate, that we do not have to worry for quite a while. Just 1 per cent of the huge mass of the sun could maintain the heat of the sun for about 150 billion years!

It is rather hard for us to realize that our sun is merely just another star in the sky. This is probably because we think of the stars as looking so tiny. The sun looks larger than any star because it is only about 93 million miles from the earth. The nearest star is 25 trillion miles away!

HOW HOT IS THE SUN?

What is the temperature on the surface of the sun? Scientists believe that it is about 10,800 degrees Fahrenheit. To give you an idea of how hot this is, white-hot molten iron used in making steel reaches a temperature of about 2,600 degrees. So you see how much hotter the sun's surface is. And as for the interior of the sun, astronomers estimate it may be as hot as 36,000,000 degrees Fahrenheit!

Remember, scientists are only taking a "guess" about this, because we know almost nothing about the interior of the sun. We do know something about the composition of this star. For example, it has been learned that the sun contains more than 60 of the chemical elements present in the earth. But it is hard to study the sun's interior because the sun is surrounded by four layers of gaseous matter.

In 1610, soon after the telescope was invented, Galileo became the first man to see spots on the sun. Through the telescope the sunspots look like dark holes in the sun's white disk.

WHAT ARE SUNSPOTS?

Sunspots may be observed on almost any clear day. They vary greatly in size. Some appear like mere specks on the sun's surface. One very large spot was about 90,000 miles long and 60,000 miles wide. Groups of sunspots are known to measure 200,000 miles in length!

Astronomers are pretty sure that sunspots are electrical in nature because of certain effects they produce. One astronomer has shown that

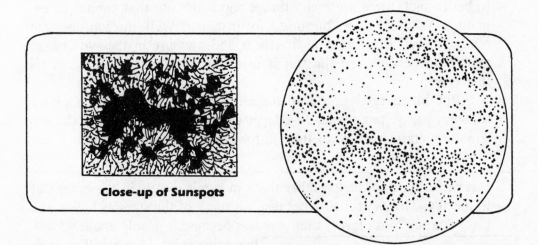

Close-up of Sunspots

they are tremendous whirls of electrified matter that come bursting out from the interior of the sun in pairs like the ends of a U-shaped tunnel.

Sunspots, or their release of electrical energy, send beams of negatively charged electrons shooting into space. Some of these electrons enter the earth's atmosphere and produce certain electrical effects.

One of these effects is the "aurora borealis" (or Northern Lights). Electrical energy from sunspots also disturbs radio transmission. These electrons also seem to increase the amount of ozone in the upper atmosphere. This extra ozone may absorb more of the sun's heat than usual, so sunspots may have a bearing on our weather.

Most sunspots last only a few days, but some last two months or more. They increase in number, then diminish, in a regular cycle which runs about 21 1/5 years. Records of sunspots have now been kept for more than 100 years and we are still learning about what they are and how they affect us.

In ancient times, the moon was worshipped as a goddess who ruled the night. Since then, man has learned a great deal about the moon, especially due to space flights by the United States and the Soviet Union, and

WHY DOES THE MOON SHINE?

the *Apollo* moon landings, which enabled astronauts to collect moon soil and rocks for scientific study.

But there is no mystery at all as to why the moon shines. It is a satellite of the earth. That is, it is a small body that revolves around it, just as the earth revolves around the sun.

The only reason we can see the moon from earth, or that it "shines," is because light from the sun strikes its surface and is reflected to us. Strangely enough, we can only see one side of the moon from the earth. This is because the moon rotates on its axis in the same length of time it takes for it to make its journey around the earth. Of course, man has already "seen" the other side in photographs, taken when instruments landed on the other side of the moon.

Since the moon has no atmosphere, or air, that light from the sun which hits it has rather interesting effects. For about 14 days, the surface of the moon is heated by the direct rays of the sun to a temperature above that of boiling water. The other half of the lunar month, it is exposed to the cold of a long, dark night.

There is gravity on or in every single object that exists in the universe. For gravity is simply the force which pulls every object in the universe toward every other object in the universe.

IS THERE GRAVITY ON THE MOON?

But the force of gravity depends on two things: the mass of the objects involved, and their distance from each other. For example, there is a force of attraction between you and the earth. But the earth is so enormous compared to you, that it pulls on you. The force of this pull is what you weigh at the earth's surface. But if you were twice as far from the center of the earth as you are now (or 4,000 miles in the air), you would weigh only one-quarter of what you weigh here on earth.

The moon is a huge object but compared to the earth it is rather small. The moon weighs only 1/81 as much as the earth. So its gravity, or pull, on its surface is much less than that of the earth. In fact, it is only one-sixth as strong as that of the earth.

On the moon, an astronaut's weight is only one-sixth of his weight on earth. When he jumps, while moving about, he can jump six times as high. And, as Alan B. Shepard, Jr. demonstrated during the *Apollo 14* mission, a golf ball can be driven six times as far—because the pull of the moon's surface is so weak.

What is the weather anyway? It is simply what the air or atmosphere is like at any time. No matter what the air is—cold, cool, warm, hot, calm, breezy, windy, dry, moist, or wet—that's weather.

WHAT MAKES THE WEATHER?

Weather may be any combination of different amounts of heat, moisture, and motion in the air. And it changes from hour to hour, day to day, season to season, and even from year to year.

The daily changes are caused by storms and fair weather moving over the earth. The seasonal changes are due to the turning of the earth around the sun. Why weather changes from year to year is still not known, however.

The most important thing to "cause" weather is the heating and cooling of the air. Heat causes the winds as well as the different way in which water vapor appears in the atmosphere.

Humidity, the amount of water vapor in the air, combined with the temperature, causes many weather conditions. Clouds are a kind of weather condition, and they are formed when water vapor condenses high above the ground.

When the cloud droplets grow larger and become too heavy to be held up by the air currents, they fall to the ground and we have the weather known as rain. If the raindrops fall through a layer of air which is below freezing, the drops freeze and our weather is snow.

One of the ways the weather forecaster studies the weather is to look at the "fronts" that exist. Fronts are boundary lines between the cold air moving southward from the north, and the warm air moving from the tropics. Most of the severe storms which cause rain, snow, and other bad weather are in some way related to these fronts.

Sometimes when we are outdoors, a sudden and mysterious thing takes place. A wind begins to blow. We cannot see it, but we feel it, and we have no idea what started it.

WHAT MAKES A WIND?

A wind is simply the motion of air over the earth. What causes the air to move? All winds are caused by one thing—a change in temperature. Whenever air is heated it expands. This makes it lighter, and lighter air rises. As the warm air rises, cooler air flows in to take its place. And this movement of air is wind!

There are two kinds of winds, those that are part of a world-wide system of winds, and local winds. The major wind systems of the world begin at the Equator, where the sun's heat is greatest.

Here the heat rises to high altitudes and is pushed off toward the North and South poles. When it has journeyed about one-third of the distance to the poles, it has cooled and begins to fall back to earth. Some of this air returns to the Equator to be heated again, and some continues on to the poles.

These types of winds, which tend to blow in the same general directino all year round, are called "prevailing winds." But these world-wide winds are often broken up by local winds which blow from different directions.

Local winds may be caused by the coming of cold air masses with high pressure, or warmer air masses with low pressure. Local winds usually do not last long. After a few hours, or at most a few days, the prevailing wind pattern is present again.

Other local winds are caused by the daily heating and cooling off of the ground. Land and sea breezes are examples of this kind of wind. In the daytime, the cool air over the ocean moves inland as the sea breeze. At night, the ocean is warmer than the ground, so the cooler air moves out to sea as the land breeze.

Of course we are all quite accustomed to thunderstorms. These are usually local storms. But there are certain kinds of storms that may cover thousands of square miles. One such type is called a "cyclonic storm" or

HOW DO TORNADOES START?

"cyclone." In a cyclone, the winds blow toward the center of an area of low pressure.

A curious thing about them is that the winds blow in spiral fashion. In the Northern Hemisphere such storms turn counterclockwise, in the Southern Hemisphere they turn clockwise!

A tornado is simply a special kind of cyclone. A tornado arises when the conditions that cause ordinary thunderstorms are unusually violent. There is an updraft of air. There are winds blowing in opposite directions around this rising air. This starts a whirling effect that is narrow and very violent. When this happens, centrifugal force throws the air away from the center. And this leaves a core of low pressure at the center.

This low-pressure core acts like a powerful vacuum on everything

it passes. This is one of the destructive things about a tornado. It can actually suck the walls of a house outward in such a way that the house will collapse. The other destructive thing about a tornado is the high winds that may blow around the edges of a whirl. These winds can reach 300 miles per hour and blow anything down.

There are many people who actually tremble with fear at the sound of a clap of thunder during a thunderstorm. There is absolutely no reason to have any fear of thunder. By the time the sound of thunder reaches you,

IS THUNDER DANGEROUS?

the bolt of electricity which caused it has already done its work. You hear the thunder after the lightning flash simply because sound travels much more slowly than light.

Should you be afraid of lightning? Well, there is no question that lightning can cause damage, and in some rare cases it has even been known to kill people. But your chances of being struck by lightning are quite small.

Lightning, of course, is a form of electricity, and this is what can make it dangerous. It is a giant spark of electricity that we see as a bright flash of light. It may jump across the space between two clouds, or from cloud to earth, or even from earth to cloud!

During a storm, different electrical charges (positive or negative) are built up by the clouds and the earth. When the difference between the charges becomes great enough, a spark—which is lightning—jumps the space between.

During and after an electrical discharge, currents of air expand and contract. The expanding and contracting currents violently collide, and produce the noise we call "thunder."

One of the most unusual weather conditions we can experience is a hailstorm. It is quite a thing to see and hear hailstones coming down, sometimes with such force that great damage is done. Animals, and even men, have been killed by hail!

WHAT CAUSES HAIL?

A hailstorm usually occurs during the warm weather and is accompanied in many cases by thunder, lightning, and rain. Hail is formed when raindrops freeze while passing through a belt of cold air on their way to earth.

Single raindrops form very small hailstones. But an interesting thing can happen to such a raindrop. As it falls as a hailstone, it may meet a strong rising current of air. So it is carried up again to the level where raindrops are falling. New drops begin to cling to the hailstone. And as it falls once more through the cold belt, these new drops spread into a layer around it and freeze, and now we have larger hailstones.

This rising and falling of the hailstone may be repeated time after time until it has added so many layers that its weight is heavy enough to overcome the force of the rising current of air. Now it falls to the ground.

In this way hailstones measuring three or four inches in diameter and weighing as much as a pound are sometimes built up. Snow, too, freezes around hailstones when they are carried into regions where it is forming. So the hailstones are frequently made up of layers of ice and snow.

Frozen rain is sometimes called hail, but it is really "sleet"! And soft hail which sometimes falls in winter is only a form of snow.

Snow is really nothing more than frozen water. Then why doesn't it look like ice?

There are a large number of ice crystals in each snowflake, and

WHAT IS SNOW?

the reflection of light from all the surfaces of the crystals makes it look white.

Snow begins to be formed when water vapor in the atmosphere freezes. Tiny crystals are formed that are clear and transparent. Since there are currents in the air, these tiny crystals are carried up and down in the atmosphere. They fall and rise as different air currents move them along.

While this is happening, the crystals begin to gather around a nucleus, so that in time there may be a hundred or more gathered together. When this group of ice crystals is big enough, it floats down toward the ground. We call this collection of ice crystals a "snowflake."

Some crystals are flat and some are like a column of needles. But regardless of the shape, snow crystals always have six sides or angles. The branches of any single snowflake are always identical, but the arrangement of the branches is different in every case. No two snowflakes are ever exactly alike.

Did you know that snow is not always white? In many parts of the world red, green, blue, and even black snow has been seen! The reason for the different colors is that sometimes there are tiny fungi in the air, or dust is floating about, and this is collected by the snow as it falls.

Because snow contains so much air, it is a poor conductor of heat. That is why a "blanket" of snow can protect dormant vegetation in the ground and why igloos and snow huts can be made of blocks of snow and keep people inside quite warm.

Everybody knows that Columbus "discovered America." Then why wasn't it named after him?

The reason for this might be considered an accident of fate. When

WHY IS OUR CONTINENT CALLED "AMERICA"?

Columbus made his first journey, he sighted land early in the morning of October 12, 1492. Columbus went ashore, took possession in the names of King Ferdinand and Queen Isabella of Spain, and named the land San Salvador. That land however, was not the mainland of the continent. It is what we now call Watling Island, in the Bahamas. Columbus actually thought he had reached India (which was his goal), so he called the natives Indians.

Columbus cruised on, looking for Japan. Instead he discovered Cuba and Hispaniola (Haiti and the Dominican Republic today). On March 14, 1493, Columbus returned to Spain.

On his second voyage, which started on September 24, 1493, Columbus discovered several of the Virgin Islands, Puerto Rico, and Jamaica. But he was still determined to find India. On his third voyage, in 1498, he discovered Trinidad and touched South America. But he thought he had found a series of islands.

Another explorer, Amerigo Vespucci, meanwhile was claiming that he had been the first to reach the mainland of South America. This was on June 16, 1497. (Many experts believe that Vespucci did not really make his voyage until 1499.)

On a trip in 1501, Vespucci sailed along the coast of South America and wrote letters saying he had found a new continent. His information was used by a German map maker—and in his maps he used the name "America" (after Amerigo Vespucci) for the new continent. And that name has been used ever since!

Stamp collecting, or philately, has been a hobby of millions of people all over the world for about 100 years. The United States Post Office has even established a special department to help stamp collectors!

WHY DO PEOPLE COLLECT STAMPS?

Of course many people collect stamps to make money. But you have to know a great deal about stamps to make big profits this way. In fact, many "collectors" never make money on stamps because they have mistaken ideas about them. They may think age alone makes a stamp valuable. Or they may see a strange stamp and think it is scarce and valuable.

Stamp collecting can be a very educational hobby. Every picture on a stamp was selected for some particular reason. Each has some bit of knowledge to give concerning the country from which it came.

The most valuable stamps, of course, are the scarcest ones. Usually there is some peculiar circumstance connected with the very scarce and valuable stamps. For instance, in certain United States post offices in 1847, there occurred a shortage of five-cent stamps. The postmasters merely cut ten-cent stamps in half, each part paying five cents postage. Today these halves are worth several hundred dollars each!

Errors occur in printing stamps, and such errors increase the value of stamps. In 1918, the first United States airmail stamps went on sale. A sheet of them sold for 24 cents each. In a certain post office, the clerk sold such a sheet at the regular price. What he did not notice was that on this particular sheet the airplane happened to have been printed upside down. Later, each of those stamps was worth $2,000!

Flags of one sort or another have been used in war since earliest times. But when the design of our flag was approved on June 14, 1777, the idea of a national flag was still very new. Most European nations were fighting

WHAT ARE SOME RULES FOR DISPLAYING OUR FLAG?

under the private flags of their kings. But after the United States had chosen a national flag, many other nations followed our example.

Since the flag is the symbol of our nation, it must be treated with reverence. There are a great many rules regarding the display of our flag, but all of them have this idea of reverence to our national symbol in mind. Here are a few of these rules of "flag etiquette":

The flag must always be flown right side up, unless used as a signal of distress. No flag must ever be flown above the flag of the United States on the same staff. When the flag is carried in procession with other flags, it must always be on the right of the line of march.

The flag should be hoisted briskly at sunrise, and lowered slowly at sunset. It should be saluted as it is being hoisted and lowered. The flag must never be used for coverings or drapery except when it is used to cover a casket.

The flag must never be allowed to touch the ground. It can be flown at half-mast as a sign of mourning. In such a case, it must first be run up to the top of the staff as usual, then slowly lowered.

The flag of the United States may be dipped at sea in a salute to a passing vessel, but it should never be dipped on land to any flag or any person. After the flag has been lowered, it is carefully folded into the shape of a three-cornered hat, to symbolize the hats worn by the soldiers of the American Revolution.

The taking of a census by a government is as old as the custom of collecting taxes and raising armies. In early times, the ruler's only object in taking a census was to discover how many people he could send to the

WHY IS THE CENSUS TAKEN?

wars or how much money he could get. Since the people suffered from the census, they did all in their power to make it incorrect.

In most countries, fairly simple questions are asked in a census—the age of the people living in a house, the relationship of these people, their birthplaces and nationality, their jobs and for whom they work. Some questions ask about date of marriage and number of children. Figures about agriculture may also be included, such as acres of land and kinds of livestock owned.

After all the information is gathered, the figures are totaled and separated according to sections or classes. They then become available and helpful to many agencies. For example, a total of age groups can be useful to governments in figuring out how many schools will be needed at a certain time, or in estimating future costs of pensions.

The census shows whether the population is increasing or decreasing. It shows the movement of population to the city or the country. It reveals whether social conditions are improving or growing worse. It tells which industries are advancing and which are slowing up.

Where office holders are elected on the basis of population, a census helps decide the number of office holders from each section. It helps the government in making laws, and it helps business, social, and economic agencies in conducting their affairs and making their plans.

The Alamo is a building in San Antonio, Texas. It is actually the chapel of the Mission San Antonio de Valero, which was founded by Franciscans in 1718. A popular name for it became "the Alamo mission,"

WHAT WAS THE ALAMO?

because it stood in a grove of cottonwood trees and the Spanish name for this tree is *alamo*.

The mission originally consisted of the chapel, a convent yard, convent and hospital building, and a plaza, all surrounded by a strong wall. When the Indians disappeared from this region, the mission was abandoned, and after 1793, it was sometimes used as a fort.

In 1835, a group of United States settlers in Texas revolted against Mexico. Texas at that time was part of one of the Mexican states. Many Americans from others parts of the United States came to help these men in their fight. Among them was a man called Davy Crockett.

Late in 1835, the Texans captured San Antonio and began to use the Alamo as a fort. The Mexican general, Antonio López de Santa Anna, marched on San Antonio with about 4,000 men. In the Alamo

were about 180 men. They were led by Col. William Travis and Col. James Bowie.

On February 23, 1836, the Mexicans surrounded the fort but were held off for 13 days. On March 6, 1836, they finally blasted a hole in the wall of the Alamo. As Mexican troops poured into the mission, the Texans continued to fight with knives and bayonets.

More than 500 Mexicans were killed, but the battle was soon over. There were not enough Texans to hold the fort. Five men were taken prisoner and later shot. "Remember the Alamo!" became the battle cry of the Texas army. Six weeks after the fall of the Alamo, the Texans, under Sam Houston, defeated Santa Anna's army and captured him in the Battle of San Jacinto.

The way we live in our society is to divide ourselves into families. Our immediate family and our relatives are our "group." But there are many primitive tribes and people who divide themselves differently.

WHAT IS A TOTEM POLE?

Among such people there are "clans," and all members of a clan are considered to be related. This relationship may be real, or they may just decide to call themselves related.

These clans usually have an "ancestor," who may be a kind of mythical human being, and the deeds of this ancestor are glorified through the ages. Or this "ancestor" may be an animal or even a plant or natural object!

Usually, the clan is descended either from an ancestor who had a special relationship with a certain animal, or from the animal itself. In such cases, the clan takes its name from the animal, and some symbol of the animal becomes the badge or "totem" of the group. The animal is called "the totem animal." Such a group is known as a "totemic clan."

Many of these clans have a totem pole. On this pole are carvings in color. They may show the totem animal or ancestor and other beings important in the story of the clan. The totem pole is usually set up in the village to give the clan prestige and to show their pride in their ancestor.

People who live in such totemic clans have different practices in different parts of the world. As a rule, members of the same clan are not allowed to marry. The children belong to the mother's clan, and not the father's.

Ever since the time of ancient Greece, stories have been told about the lost island, or continent, of Atlantis. It was thought to be a very large island in the Atlantic Ocean, just west of the Rock of Gibraltar. It was

WHAT WAS THE LOST CONTINENT OF ATLANTIS?

believed to be a perfect place—a kind of paradise.

According to legends, Atlantis was a powerful kingdom whose people conquered all of southwestern Europe and northwestern Africa. They were finally defeated by the Athenians from Greece.

The people of Atlantis then became wicked. As a punishment, the island was swallowed up by the ocean. This legend is told in the *Timaeus,* written in the 300's B.C. by the Greek philosopher Plato. The island was supposed to have been lost more than 9,000 years before Plato's time.

During the Middle Ages, the stories about Atlantis were believed to be true. In the fourteenth and fifteen centuries, many voyages were made to try to find Atlantis. The stories may have come from some true happenings. Perhaps a voyager brought back tales of his discovery of a new and strange land, and in time these tales became part of the legend of Atlantis.

Even today there are people who firmly believe there was such a place. According to the man who is considered the greatest expert on Atlantis by these believers, Atlantis was a place where man first became civilized. He also believes many of the gods worshipped by ancient peoples were really the kings and queens of Atlantis, and that the Atlanteans were the first to manufacture iron and have an alphabet.

If you ever make a trip to Italy, one of the most fascinating sights to see is Pompeii. For here is a city almost 2,000 years old that you will be able to see and study in greater detail, and better preserved, than almost

WHAT WAS POMPEII?

any other ancient city.

Why is this so? On August 24, in the year A.D. 79, there was a great eruption of Mount Vesuvius, a volcano in southern Italy. The lava, stones, and ashes thrown up by the volcano completely buried two nearby towns.

The town of Herculaneum, about two miles away, was deeply covered by a stream of mud which flowed down the slope of the mountain. Pompeii, farther along the coast, was buried by the rain of ashes and pebbles of light pumice stone. These fell over Pompeii in a dry state, and the mass which covered the city was from 18 to 20 feet thick.

When water came down on top of this, the material became like clay or plaster of Paris. As a result, objects that were caught in it made molds of the material, and the two towns were remarkably preserved underneath!

Survivors of this disaster returned to the towns, and by digging down and tunneling were able to remove most of the valuable objects, including slabs of marble that were on the large buildings.

In the Middle Ages, this place and everything about it was forgotten. In 1594, an underground aqueduct was started here, and the ruins were rediscovered. But it took until 1763 before any real excavating was done, and it has been carried on ever since. But nearly half of Pompeii is still buried!

This is certainly a strange name for a body of water—but no other sea in the world has had such a variety of names!

It was first called "dead sea" by ancient Greek writers. The Hebrews called it "the salt sea," among other names. Arab writers called it "the stinking sea."

WHAT IS THE DEAD SEA?

What is so strange about this sea? It is really a large, narrow salt lake that lies between Jordan and Israel. It lies in a deep trough, or "rift," which is a deep depression in this area.

The Dead Sea is about 48 miles long, and ranges from 3 to 11 miles in width. Now comes the amazing part. The Dead Sea is the lowest body of water in the world. The surface of this sea is about 1,300 feet below sea level. The southern part of the sea is very shallow, but in the north the depth is about 1,300 feet.

There are no streams flowing out of the Dead Sea. But into it drain the Jordan River from the north and many smaller streams from the surrounding slopes. There is only one way the surplus water is carried away—by evaporation. This leaves behind in the water a large concentration of minerals, such as salt, potash, magnesium, chloride, and bromine.

The Dead Sea is the world's saltiest body of water. The water is about six times as salty as that of the ocean! There are so many minerals concentrated in this sea, that a man swimming in it will float with his head and shoulders out of the water at all times! These minerals can be valuable to man. In fact, it is estimated that dissolved in this water are about two million tons of potash, which is used in making artificial fertilizers.

The Dead Sea is one of the strangest bodies of water to be found on the earth. Millions of years ago, the Dead Sea was about 1,400 feet higher than it is today, and so was on a higher level than the Mediterranean Sea.

IS THERE ANY LIFE IN THE DEAD SEA? At that time, life did exist in it. But then a great dry period came, and so much of it evaporated, that the sea gradually shrank in size to its present state.

One of the most amazing things about the Dead Sea is the amount of salt it contains. Normal ocean water contains about 4 to 6 per cent of salts. The Dead Sea contains 23 to 25 per cent of salts! If you taste this water, it is not only salty, but it may make you nauseous because of the chloride of magnesium in it. The water also has a smooth, oily feeling because of the chloride of calcium in it.

No animal life can exist in the Dead Sea. The Jordan River flows into it, bringing fish along with it. But the fish die, furnishing food for the sea birds.

When we try to learn of the accomplishments of ancient man, we usually have to search or dig for evidence. But there is a case where ancient man has left all the evidence standing in a huge structure, and we still cannot

WHAT IS STONEHENGE? figure out what it is, what it was used for, and who built it!

This is Stonehenge. It consists of large, standing stones in a circular setting, surrounded by an earthwork, and located near Salisbury, England. As long ago as the year 1136, it was written that the stones were magically transported from Ireland by Merlin. Of course, this was only a legend. More recently, it was believed that Stonehenge was put up by the Druids, who were priests in ancient England. But there is actually no reason to believe this is so.

Stonehenge has a somewhat complicated structure. On the outside is a circular ditch, with an entrance gap. Then there is a bank of earth.

Inside the bank is a ring of 56 pits. Between these and the stones in the center, are two more rings of pits.

The stone setting consists of two circles and two horseshoes of upright stones. Then there are separate stones which have been given names, such as the Altar stone, the Slaughter stone, two Station stones, and the Hele stone.

In most of the holes that have been excavated, cremated human bones have been found. By studying the pottery and objects found, and by making radioactive-carbon tests, it has been estimated that parts of Stonehenge date back to about 1848 B.C., and possibly 275 years earlier or later than this date.

Part of Stonehenge is aligned so that the rising sun in midsummer is seen at a certain point, but nobody is sure if this was intentional.

So this huge and remarkable structure, which may be 4,000 years old, still remains a fascinating mystery!

The proper name of this great and famous statue is "Liberty Enlightening the World," and it stands in New York harbor as a symbol of freedom.

The statue was a gift from the people of France to the people of the

WHEN WAS THE STATUE OF LIBERTY BUILT?

United States, but there were many problems involved with the presentation of this magnificent gift. In 1865, a French historian named Edouard de Laboulaye proposed that his country present a memorial to the United States on the 100th anniversary of the signing of the Declaration of Independence. The Franco-Prussian War intervened, and nothing was done about this idea for some time.

Then in 1874, a sculptor named Frédéric Bartholdi was sent to New York to confer with American authorities about the idea. As he sailed into the harbor, he got the inspiration for a huge "Goddess of Liberty" to stand at the gateway to the New World.

The Franco-American Union was formed to collect the money this would cost. The total cost of the statue itself was contributed by the people of France. The people of the United States contributed about $250,000 for the pedestal on which the statue stands. It was dedicated on October 28, 1886, ten years later than had been originally planned.

The total weight of the Statue of Liberty is 225 tons. It is nearly 152 feet tall and stands on a pedestal 150 feet above the water. The pedestal rests upon a 23,500 ton concrete foundation that reaches down 20 feet to bedrock.

Maybe you did not even know the Nile River had a "riddle." Well, it is something that has puzzled people for thousands of years, and it has to do with a very curious event.

WHAT IS "THE RIDDLE OF THE NILE"?

Every year in Egypt, the Nile River starts to rise in July and continues to rise until October, when its level is about 25 feet above the level in May. During the high-water season, the Nile spills over its banks and deposits fertile silt on the fields along its course.

What makes this rising of the river mysterious is that there is practically no rainfall in Egypt! So for hundreds of years people have wondered what makes the Nile rise so regularly each year. This "riddle of the Nile" was not solved until late in the nineteenth century.

The Nile is the longest river in the world. It flows over 4,000 miles from south to north in the northeastern part of Africa, mainly in Sudan and Egypt. The yearly flooding of the Nile has made its valley a fertile ribbon in a hot, dry, barren wasteland, and people have lived here for thousands of years.

There are two main streams and sources of the Nile River—the White Nile and the Blue Nile. The White Nile has its origin at Lake

Victoria in Uganda. It has a fairly even flow throughout the year, so it cannot cause the annual rise of the Nile River. During April and May, when the water in the lower Nile is at its lowest, 85 per cent of the water is coming from the White Nile.

But what about the Blue Nile? It rises in Ethiopia. In the Ethiopian Mountains there are heavy rains and melting snows. And when these come down every year, they cause the Nile River to rise and overflow. And that is the answer to "the riddle of the Nile"!

It is quite an amazing experience to be in a city where most of the "highways" are canals! But unlike most cities, Venice's roadways, the canals, were there before the city was built!

WHY DOES VENICE HAVE CANALS?

Venice is built on a group of mud banks that formed over 100 small islands at the head of the Adriatic Sea. All buildings are erected on pilings driven into this mud. In between the mud banks are strips of the sea, and these are the famous canals of Venice!

In this city, transportation is either by boat or on foot. There are no cars or carts allowed inside the old town. There are numerous narrow alleys and little bridges which span the canals. And everywhere one sees that small boat known as "the gondola." The gondolier, the driver of the boat, stands on a platform in the rear of the boat and propels it with a long pole.

Venice is a very old city. Long before the Huns swept down through Italy in about the middle of the fifth century, there were people already living on the little islands of the lagoon. After a while, 12 lagoon townships were formed. This was the beginning of the state of Venice, within which developed gradually the city now known as Venice.

In 1450, Venice was the head of a huge colonial empire and was the chief sea power in the world. Beginning with the sixteenth century, new trade routes were discovered and the trade of Venice began to decline.

In the following years, Venice was involved in many wars, lost its empire, and was practically destroyed by its enemies. In 1866, Venice voted to become part of the kingdom of Italy.

Today, Venice is one of the great artistic centers of Europe and is beginning to regain its position as a great port.

On Easter Day in 1722, a Dutch admiral called Jacob Roggeveen landed on a grass-covered island in the South Pacific. He named it Easter Island and discovered it to be a very strange place indeed.

WHAT ARE THE EASTER ISLAND STATUES?

The island was more than 1,000 miles from the nearest inhabited land. There were over 2,000 natives living on the island, and they were a dark Polynesian people. But the most curious thing of all was what this explorer saw on the island.

All along the coast he found large, stone heads. They had long faces and exceptionally long ears. Some of these statues had hands and

some wore hats that were made of red lava. He soon discovered that these statues not only appeared along the coast, but they were at scattered points inland. Many were found partially finished in the quarries where they had been carved.

Primitive peoples all over the world have various art forms, usually connected with their religion, but nothing like these statues had ever been found anywhere else! And the truth is, they still remain a mystery. How could these heavy figures, some of which weigh about 50 tons, be moved from the quarries to their places? What form of transportation could the primitive people have developed?

No one knows! It is believed that the statues were probably connected with primitive religious practices and burial customs of the people. And many of the statues were purposely broken during native wars that took place on the island during and after the eighteenth century. But even the natives living on the island today cannot explain the meaning of the huge statues!

Today the island is governed by Chile. Except for a small section reserved for the natives, the entire island is used for grazing cattle and sheep. The island is only about 13 miles long and 7 miles wide at its broadest point.

Before the year 1700, many different groups of Indians lived who constructed mounds of earth, clay, shell, and stone. A popular name for them is the Mound Builders.

WHO WERE THE MOUND BUILDERS?

The first kind of mounds built by these Indians were burial mounds, built over the graves of the dead. They were made of earth, clay, shells, or stones. These cone-shaped or dome-shaped burial mounds ranged from several feet in height and ten feet in diameter to a size like the Miamisburg mound in Ohio. This was about 68 feet high and 250 feet in diameter. It was the custom of the Mound Builders to bury certain small, personal ornaments or utensils with the body.

After the custom of mound-burial was begun, a different kind of mound began to be constructed—an effigy mound. They were called effigies because they were built in the form of animals: bears, deer, buffalo, birds, and serpents. Most of them were found in Wisconsin and many of these contained burials.

A somewhat different style of effigy mound is found in Ohio. It was associated with the Adena and possibly the Hopewell Indians. The most famous is the Great Serpent Mound in Adams County, Ohio. This mound is four feet high and spreads out in zigzag fashion for more than 1,330 feet. It looks like a great snake with a triangular head. Just in front of the head is an oval mound. This may be a frog or an egg which the snake is about to swallow.

The most recent type of mound built by these Indians was the flat-topped pyramidal type. It had a temple on top and a ramp or stairway led to the temple.

Mounds are found over a wide area between the Great Lakes and the Gulf of Mexico, and between the Atlantic Ocean and the Great Plains of the West. Most of the mounds are in the Mississippi Valley.

At one time, people believed that there lived on this earth with us all kinds of strange beings who had magical powers. Sometimes they were called fairies, and sometimes they had special names, depending on their power or on the country where they were supposed to live.

WHAT IS A LEPRECHAUN?

Leprechauns were the fairy shoemakers of Ireland. They were little old wrinkled men, not even as big as a new-born child. In Scotland, similar fairies about two feet high were called brownies. A brownie chose some house to serve and, coming at night, scrubbed and cleaned and did all sorts of work. All he would take in payment was a bowl of cream and a bit of white bread.

In England, the very smallest fairies were called pixies. They would wear green jackets and red caps and dance to the music of crickets and grasshoppers. In France, they were called fees and in Scandinavia, white elves. They lived in the woods and fields and a mortal could find his way to their home only on one of the four magical nights of the year—Midsummer Eve, May Eve, Christmas Eve, or Halloween.

Fairies that were bigger in size had different names. For instance, if they were from 18 inches to the size of small children, they were called goblins. In Germany they were called gnomes and dwarfs. And in Scandinavia they were called trolls.

Sometimes there were human-sized fairies, and they were hard to tell from mortals. In Germany, if you met a man with green teeth he was a nix, or water spirit. When nixes ventured on land, some bit of their clothing was always wet.

Of course it was considered very difficult to know the real size of a fairy because they were so seldom seen.

Sometimes a man, or a thing he does, captures the imagination of a country. His deed may not be decisive in his country's history, but he becomes a kind of national hero. Such a man was George Armstrong Custer.

WHAT WAS CUSTER'S LAST STAND?

Custer graduated from the United States Military Academy in 1861, and joined the Union forces in the Civil War. He became one of the most daring cavalry leaders in the Union Army. When the war ended, Custer was made a lieutenant colonel in the regular army and went to Kansas to fight Indians.

In 1876, Sioux Indians were attacking the Western settlements. A large United States force was sent against them. Custer, with about 600 men, was sent on a scouting expedition. On June 24, 1876, he was told that Indians under the leadership of Sitting Bull were encamped on the Little Big Horn River in Montana. Custer's scouts reported only a few hundred Indians, but the number turned out to be more than 2,500.

Custer then made the mistake of dividing his small force in hopes of surrounding the enemy. One unit attacked and then retreated when it saw the size of the Indian force. A second never got into the fight. With about 225 men, Custer attacked the Indians. In hand-to-hand fighting all of his little band was killed. This desperate fight they made became known as "Custer's Last Stand."

The tragedy stunned the country. Today, a monument and national cemetery mark the site of this battle. Custer himself is buried at West Point.

Usually you hear of Mason and Dixon's Line as a sort of boundary between the North and South in the United States. People say that a certain way of life exists south of the line, and another way of life exists north of it.

WHAT IS MASON'S AND DIXON'S LINE?

Here is how Mason and Dixon's Line came into existence. When the kings of England were giving away land in America, there were no accurate maps of the continent. As a result, the descriptions of the grants were confused and there were many disputes. In one case, some of the same land was given to William Penn of Pennsylvania and to Lord Baltimore of Maryland.

In the grant to Penn, the southern boundary of Pennsylvania was designated as the parallel marking "the beginning of the 40th degree of northern latitude." And the northern boundary of Maryland was defined as a line "which lieth under the 40th degree of northern latitude."

So after much dispute, two astronomers were sent from England to survey the boundary in 1763. They were Charles Mason and Jeremiah Dixon, and they spent four years marking a boundary 244 miles long. They even brought over milestones from England, and set them up on the eastern part of the line. Every fifth stone had the arms of Baltimore on one side and the arms of Penn on the other side. But many of the stones were never set up because it was so hard to transport them.

The British government approved this line in 1769, and Mason and Dixon's Line became the boundary of Maryland and Pennsylvania. North of Mason and Dixon's Line was a land of small farms and growing cities. South of it were fewer cities and many large cotton and tobacco plantations. By 1804, all of the states north of the line had abolished slavery.

So Mason and Dixon's Line became more than a symbol. It actually divided two ways of life in the United States.

The first "Americans" came to America so long ago that we cannot really know as much as we would like to know about their earliest history. But this is what most authorities think happened.

WHERE DID THE AMERICAN INDIANS COME FROM?

About 12,000 years ago, bands of hunters on foot wandered into a strange new land, following herds of elk and caribou. The land these early hunters came from was probably Siberia. They crossed over to Alaska where the continents of Asia and North America are closest together at the narrow strip of water now called Bering Strait.

For thousands of years more hunters came to North America. They did not come all at once, but came in small family groups. Although they came from the same homeland and were originally alike, they came

Eastern   Plains   Northwest Coast

WOODLANDS IROQUOIS   **SIOUX**   **TLINGIT**

54

over a period of thousands of years and thus the groups differed in many ways. They differed in language, in appearance, in customs, in ways of making a living, and in the way they adapted themselves to life in the new land.

They all had straight, black hair and high cheekbones. They were all dark-skinned, but their shadings varied. The skins of some had a reddish tinge and so these people were often called "red men."

They used the same sort of weapons and tools, and methods to provide themselves with food, clothing, and shelter. But they used different materials to satisfy these needs.

The biggest differences that developed among these people were a result of where they settled to live. There were five main living centers where these people settled: the Northwest Coast, the California region, the Southwest, the Eastern Woodlands, and the Plains. The tribes that developed in each of these centers were quite different from each other —though they were all what we came to know as "Indians."

Practically everybody has heard of or read stories about King Arthur and his Knights of the Round Table. They are not considered to be true stories, but legends. What are they based on?

DID KING ARTHUR EVER EXIST?

Well, no one knows who King Arthur really was. Most writers of history believe that there was a great chief of one of the tribes in Britain around the year A.D. 500, and the legends have grown up about this man.

King Arthur may have been part Roman and part British, for the Romans had ruled England for nearly 400 years. Arthur probably led a large army against the Saxon invaders.

In both Wales and Brittany, Arthur was remembered and admired. Stories about him were passed from one generation to another. Each story was more wonderful than the last. Finally, Arthur became one of the greatest heroes who ever lived. He killed horrible monsters, had great magical powers, and became a great and good king.

Nobody knows for sure just where Arthur had his castle. There are about six different places in England that claim to be the location of Camelot, his home.

The first writer to mention Arthur was an early Welsh historian who lived about the eighth century. After that first mention of Arthur, nothing was written about him for about 400 years. Then in the twelfth century, stories about King Arthur became quite common. The earliest were written in Latin, and then French and English poets began to write about him.

In the fifteenth century, Sir Thomas Malory wrote down many of the stories about Arthur in a book called *Morte d'Arthur (Death of Arthur).*

Paul Bunyan is a legendary hero of American folklore. There is probably no other figure in America about whom so many wonderful and fantastic tales have been told, and who is supposed to have done so many remarkable things.

WHO WAS PAUL BUNYAN?

There was a real man called Paul Bunyon, who lived in the early 1800's and who was a French-Canadian. He operated a lumber camp, and the people who worked for him told marvelous tales of his bravery and strength.

The American lumberjacks adopted him as a sort of hero who symbolized their own hearty and exciting life. In their tales, they had him cross the border into the United States, change his name to Bunyan, invent logging, and start on a life of great adventures and deeds. By 1860, Paul Bunyan had become a legendary American hero.

All the stories about Paul Bunyan have an element of exaggeration about them, but they are full of delightful imagination. Paul's voice was like a clap of thunder, and he could carry 20 grindstones weighing a ton apiece. By swinging his axe around him in a circle, he cut down all the trees within reach.

Paul's chief helper was an enormous blue ox named Babe. Paul and Babe together changed the map of the United States. Paul made the Great Lakes as reservoirs for Babe's drinking water. Kansas is flat because Paul hitched Babe to it and turned it over to make good corn land. When Babe lay down and rolled, Lake Superior was formed. Babe made the Mississippi River by upsetting a cart of water. Once when Paul was strolling along the Colorado River, he dragged a pick along the ground; the scratch it made formed the Grand Canyon.

For many years these stories were only spread orally. In 1914, some of them were published, and since then many other books about Paul Bunyan have come out.

If a person has some way in which he can be hurt, or some spot in which he can be wounded, he is said to have an Achilles heel.

This expression goes gack to one of the greatest heroes of Greek legends, the story of Achilles. When

WHO WAS ACHILLES?

Achilles was born, the Fates, the goddesses that controlled man's destiny, foretold that the infant would die young. Achilles' mother, Thetis, wanted to avoid this fate for her son, so she dipped him in the waters of the River Styx. This was supposed to make him invulnerable and protect him from deadly wounds.

Every part of Achilles was thus made safe against injury, except one part—the heel by which his mother held him! And later on, he was to die from a wound in the heel.

Achilles grew to be a handsome young man, swiftest of mortals in the race, and the joy of all who beheld him. Eventually Achilles became famous as the greatest of the Greek warriors during the Trojan War.

In the tenth year of the struggle, he captured a girl named Briseis. But the leader of the Greeks, Agamemnon, took the girl away from him. Achilles was furious and decided not to fight any more. The Greeks were helpless without their great hero. So they persuaded Achilles to lend his armor and his men to his friend, Patroclus.

But Patroclus was slain by the Trojan hero Hector, and the armor was captured. Then Achilles decided to obtain revenge. He became friends again with Agamemnon, and put on armor and a shield. He took the field and killed Hector. And in revenge he dragged Hector's body around the tomb of his slain friend.

Later, Hector's brother, Paris, shot a poisoned arrow at Achilles. It entered his heel, the one part of his body that had not been dipped in the Styx, and Achilles died from the wound.

Socrates has come to stand for the ideal of a wise man, yet one of his principles was that it is wise to know that your wisdom is worth nothing!

He was born in Athens, Greece, about 470 B.C. Little is known of

WHO WAS SOCRATES?

his parents or childhood. He left no writings. His disciple, the great philosopher Plato, wrote down in the form of dialogues Socrates' teachings and ideas, together with many scenes from his life.

According to Plato, Socrates spent his time in the market place of Athens talking to anybody who would listen. He liked especially to find someone with firm ideas on a subject. Socrates would draw him out with leading questions and show him he was ignorant of the subject he had been so sure about. Hence, the method of arguing by asking questions is called Socratic. His one fundamental principle was "Know thyself."

The Athenians disliked him because he upset all their former ideas. Therefore they said of him that he did not believe in the gods, or in truth, or in justice.

In the year 399 B.C., his enemies brought him to trial on the charge of having corrupted the youth of Athens and of neglecting his religious duties. No one believed the accusations and Socrates realized this. The defense he made, known as "the Apology of Socrates," was afterward written out by Plato. It was mocking and courageous. Although Socrates knew that he would be condemned to death, he said he must go on leading the same life, devoting himself to the search for truth.

In prison, Socrates passed his last day discussing with his friends the immortality of the soul. He took the cup of hemlock, the poison which was given him, without trembling and drank it. His friends burst into tears, but he begged them to be silent. He died with a smile on his lips.

It is not often that we make a hero of a robber, but Robin Hood somehow seems to be different. Everybody knows it is wrong to steal, yet Robin Hood is admired. The reason for this, of course, is that he stole from the rich and gave to the poor.

WHO WAS ROBIN HOOD?

Did Robin Hood ever actually exist? We know that he was a favorite figure in the ballads and stories of England in the fourteenth and fifteenth centuries. He was supposed to have lived in the twelfth century. In a Latin history which appeared in the year 1521, this is what was written about Robin Hood:

"About the time of Richard I, Robin Hood and Little John, the most famous of robbers, were lurking in the woods and stealing only from rich men; they killed none except those who resisted them or came to attack them. Robin kept 100 archers on the proceeds of these robberies, well trained for fighting, and not even 400 men dared to come against them.

"All England sings of the deeds of this Robin; he would not allow any woman to be hurt, nor did he ever take the goods from the poor; indeed he kept them richly supplied with the goods he stole from the abbots."

One can see how such a character must have captured the imagination of the English people of that period, because they loved chivalry and archery. Robin pleased them and they built around his name one legend after another. They made him a great sportsman, a wonderful archer, and a lover of the green woods where he lived.

There are many theories about Robin Hood. One of these suggests that he was a Saxon, and among the last of those who held out against the Normans when they conquered England. It seems certain that a Robin Hood really did exist. But it is also pretty certain that many of the stories that existed in other legends came to be told about Robin Hood.

The Incan civilization was at least 400 years old at the time Columbus discovered America.

The land of the Incas included what is now Bolivia, Peru, Ecuador,

WHO WERE THE INCAS?

and part of Argentina and Chile. In the center of the Inca Empire was Cuzco, the capital, the Sacred City of the Sun. It was the center of the only world these people knew, and to this city came caravans from every part of the empire with grain, gold and silver, fine cloth, and fresh, green coca leaves.

The Incas were stern but just rulers. They allowed the people they conquered to follow their own customs. The family was the center of government. Each group of ten families had a leader. He reported to a captain who had 50 families under him, and so on up to the Inca, who ruled the empire.

Everyone in the Inca Empire worked, except the very young and the old. Each family had a certain amount of land to farm. The people wove their own clothing, made their own shoes or sandals, their own dishes of pottery, and objects of gold and silver.

The people had no personal freedom: the Inca decided what clothes they wore, what food they ate, what work they did. The sick, poor, and old were cared for. The Incas were wonderful farmers and grew excellent crops. They built great aqueducts to bring mountain streams down to water their fields.

Many of the buildings which the Incas erected still stand. And they built unusual bridges made of vines and willow branches braided into huge ropes. The people were very skilful at weaving and pottery. They made cotton cloth so fine the Spaniards thought it was silk, and they made fine clothing of wool.

After many centuries of prosperity, the Inca Empire was divided between two half-brothers who began to fight each other. When the Spaniards came, they found it easy to conquer them and destroy the empire.

One of the most important peoples of ancient America were the Aztecs, who lived in the valley which now contains Mexico City. Long before the Europeans came from across the sea, these American Indians were making history.

WHO WERE THE AZTECS?

They had developed a way of life almost the equal of many of the European peoples. They carved their history in stone. They built temples and towers and homes of solid masonry. They were quite skilled in astronomy, law, and government, and were expert in many arts and crafts. They were in some ways a kind and gentle people. They were lovers of nature, especially birds and flowers. They also were fond of music, dancing, plays, and literature.

The Aztecs, however, had also risen to power through military abilities, and warfare was often carried on for the purpose of capturing enemies for sacrifice to their war god. The custom of sacrificing human life was shocking to the Europeans, but this developed naturally among the Aztecs because they combined religion and warfare.

The Aztecs were also called Mexica. From this, or from one of their gods, comes the word for Mexico. In 1325, 167 years before Columbus ever saw an Indian, the Aztecs, according to tradition, started to build their capital which they called Tenochtitlán. This city was later to become the capital of the Spanish and finally of the Mexican republic.

No one knows exactly where the Aztecs came from. The legends about them indicate that they came from the north. They probably arrived in the Valley of Mexico in the twelfth or thirteenth century. In these early times they were known as Tenochcas. The Toltecs, who already lived in the valley and were quite cultured, considered the Aztecs as barbaric newcomers. Because of this the Aztecs had a difficult time settling in the valley. But in time they rose to great power and ruled over the peoples of the Valley of Mexico.

About 1,200 years ago there was a group of people, the Northmen, who came from the coastal regions of Norway, Sweden, and Denmark. Their name "viking" was probably taken from the *viks,* or sounds, of

WHO WERE THE VIKINGS?

their home region. The vikings were great sailors and adventurers.

They were strong and sturdy, often with blue eyes and fair hair. At a time when the rest of Europe was terrified to sail the sea, the vikings were great explorers and traders. They preferred conquest and adventure to a life of quiet safety.

In A.D. 793, the vikings made their first attack on the English coast. From that time and up through the eleventh century, they raided the coasts of western and eastern Europe. They plundered England, Ireland, France, and Spain. They even journeyed as far south as Algiers.

Vikings discovered islands to the west of Greenland and a portion of the North American continent, which they called Vinland. A colony was attempted at Vinland and settlers remained on the continent for three years.

The Northmen had a civilization of their own. Viking ships, carriages, household dishes, and ornaments have been discovered in their graves. There were many iron deposits in viking lands and the Northmen became skilled workers in this metal.

The vikings were originally pagans. Odin and Thor were their chief gods. According to viking beliefs, the gods lived in a place called Valhalla, and heroes who died in battle were welcomed there. They also had a literature of "sagas," or stories, which were about life among the kings, chieftains, and common people.

The Northmen had a good system of law based on fairness and sportsmanship. It is even believed that the jury system we have today can be traced back to the ancient Northmen.

There are actually no such things as weeds. When a farmer plants certain seeds which he hopes will produce a valuable crop, he calls any other plant which grows up in his field and interferes with his crop a weed!

HOW DO WEEDS SPREAD?

Basically, though, weeds are plants that do harm. Some are poisonous to cattle and horses. Others injure crops by robbing them of sunlight, soil, minerals, and water. Others act as parasites, or serve as hosts to insects or plant diseases that cause harm.

Weeds are spread by various means. Some weeds are carried from place to place in fodder, in dust, in rubbish, and in manure. But most weeds that cause so much trouble do not spread because of man's carelessness. They have their own devices for spreading their seeds.

Some weeds, such as pimpernel, knotweed, dodder, and goldenrod, produce their seeds in such great quantities that some of them are likely to survive practically no matter what the conditions.

Other weeds have hairlike or winglike projections on their seeds and fruits. These make it possible for the seeds to be carried by the wind for considerable distances. Such weeds include dock, sorrel, thistle, and dandelion. Still other weeds have little hooks or spines on their seeds. These hooks catch in the fur of animals or in the clothing of man, and in this way the seeds are spread to new territory.

Some of the most successful weeds do not even spread by means of seeds. They have spreading underground stems which send up erect

branches. If the underground stem is cut, these erect branches merely become separate plants.

Because of the harm they can do, weeds are fought and controlled by man. Today there is a whole variety of chemicals that have been developed to destroy weeds or prevent them from appearing.

Air is everywhere about you. Every crack, hole, and space that is not already filled with something else is filled with air. Every time you breathe, your lungs are filled with air.

WHAT IS AIR?

Even though you cannot see air, nor taste it, nor feel it (unless the wind is blowing), air is "something." It is a substance or material which scientists call "matter." Matter may be a solid, a liquid, or a gas. The matter called "air" is almost always a gas.

In fact, air is made up of certain gases. Two of these, nitrogen and oxygen, make up 99 per cent of the air. They are always found in the same proportion of about 78 per cent nitrogen and about 21 per cent oxygen. There is also a small amount of carbon dioxide in the air which is added to it by living things. The remaining part of 1 per cent is made up of what are called rare gases: argon, neon, helium, krypton, and xenon.

The great ocean of air extends for many miles above the surface of the earth. Because air is something, gravity attracts, or holds it, to the earth. Thus air has weight. The weight of the air exerts pressure. The air presses on your whole body from all directions, just as water would if you were at the bottom of the sea.

If you climb a high mountain or go up in an airplane, there is less air above you, so the pressure is less as you go up. About eight miles up, the pressure is only one-eighth that at sea level. At 62 miles, there is almost no pressure.

All over the world, there are people who are waging "conservation" campaigns. Conservation means many things to many people.

To some it means preserving the wilderness in certain sections. To

WHAT IS CONSERVATION?

others it means preserving the wildlife. Conservation includes efforts to protect forests as well as the wise use of all natural resources.

The problem of conservation has arisen because mankind is using the world's natural resources in greater quantity and variety than ever before. As the world's population grows, and as more people live at a higher standard, there is a greater demand for resources. These resources must be "conserved" to assure that there will be enough for the future.

What do we mean by "resources"? Well, they can be divided into three basic kinds. One is renewable resources. For example, water, farmland, forests, and grazing land, even while they are being used, can be improved and renewed through good management. This would include protection from erosion, irrigation, and fertilization.

A second group of resources is not renewable. These are mainly minerals. They are used up once they are taken from the earth. These include coal, oil, and natural gas.

There are some natural resources that cannot be used up. For example, solar energy, climate, and oceans cannot be increased, decreased, or damaged by man. Man can also destroy the beauty of scenery, or cause pollution of air.

The only reason a day has 24 hours is that man has decided he would like to figure time that way.

Nothing occurs in nature or in the world that has anything to do

WHY IS THE DAY 24 HOURS?

with hours or minutes or seconds. These divisions of time were made up by man for his convenience. But something does happen that has to do with what we call a "day." And that something is the rotation of the earth on its axis from west to east. Every time it goes around once, a specific amount of time has passed. We call that time a "day."

Scientists can measure that time exactly and they use the stars to do it. Observatories have what is called "sidereal" clocks. A sidereal day begins the instant that a given star crosses a meridian and lasts until the instant that it recrosses the same meridian.

Since man has broken up the day into hours, minutes, and seconds, we can say exactly how long a sidereal day is. It is 23 hours 56 minutes and 4.09 seconds long. But it would be difficult to use a day of sidereal length for ordinary purposes, so we use a 24-hour day, with an extra day added during leap year to correct the difference.

To early people, a day meant simply the space between sunrise and sunset. The hours at night were not counted. The Greeks counted their day from sunset to sunset. For the Romans, it was from midnight to midnight.

Before clocks were invented, day and night were divided into 12 hours each. This division was not practical as the length of the two periods differs with the seasons. Today, most countries have a day which, by law, extends over the 24-hour period from midnight to midnight, following the Roman method.

Capital punishment is the inflicting of the death penalty for a crime. Where capital punishment exists, it is carried out by the government in accordance with its laws regarding crime. In the United States, the matter of capital punishment is subject to the laws of individual states.

WHAT IS CAPITAL PUNISHMENT?

It is possible to say that the death penalty is the most effective form of punishment—since it makes sure that the offender will never commit another crime. It is also considered to be a way of preventing crime, since the threat of capital punishment may frighten people who would otherwise do wrong.

But there are a great many people who believe that capital punishment is wrong. They say that man has no right to take another person's life, and they claim that it does not even help prevent crime. Such people believe that capital punishment will eventually disappear in all civilized lands.

In ancient times, when people had not yet learned how to behave in a disciplined way in society, it was probably to be expected that capital punishment existed. In Egypt and Babylonia, death might be the penalty for any action that the ruler did not like. The ancient Hebrews showed an advance in humanity by limiting the crimes punishable by death to murder, blasphemy, breaking of the Sabbath, and various social crimes.

Both the Greeks and the Romans had well-organized criminal laws which inflicted the death penalty for crimes against the state. In Athens, some of those condemned to death, among them Socrates, were forced to drink a poison made from hemlock. In Rome, criminals who were not citizens were executed by crucifixion.

During the Middle Ages, the death penalty was inflicted for even minor offenses, such as stealing a sheep or cutting down someone else's tree. It wasn't until early in the nineteenth century that civilization had advanced to the point where capital punishment was limited to major crimes of murder and high treason.

When we say "country," we usually mean an independent state that has a distinct territory and its own government.

The world's smallest independent state is Vatican City. It lies in

WHAT IS THE SMALLEST COUNTRY IN THE WORLD?

the midst of Rome, Italy, and has a total area of only 0.17 square miles! It is the place of government of the Catholic Church.

The pope, the head of Vatican City, rules through a civil governor. Vatican City has its own flag, post office, railway station, and money. It also has a telephone system and radio broadcasting station. Support for this tiny state comes chiefly from contributions made by Catholics throughout the world.

Within Vatican City there is the Vatican Palace (the pope's residence), the gardens, and the large St. Peter's Basilica. In the palace are art museums and libraries. The Vatican Library, in a separate wing, is one of the greatest in the world.

Vatican City

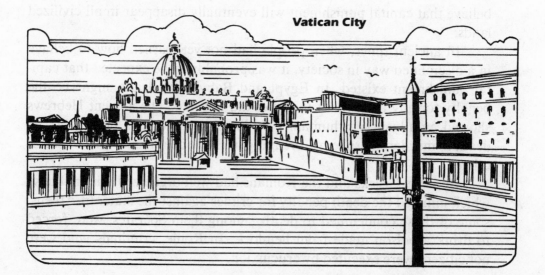

Vatican City has diplomatic relations with other countries and receives representatives from many nations.

Over the years, political control was gained by the popes over a large territory in central Italy. In 1859, this land, called the "Papal States," covered about 16,000 square miles.

In 1870, Rome was made the national capital of Italy. Against the objections of the pope, the Papal States were made part of the kingdom of Italy.

In 1929, an agreement was reached between the pope and the Italian government and the Vatican City was set up.

The eucalyptus is a native tree of Australia, where it is sometimes called "the gum tree" or "string-bark" tree. It now has been introduced into Europe, Algeria, Egypt, India, South America, and southern United States.

WHAT IS EUCALYPTUS?

The eucalyptus is one of the most striking trees in appearance. Its leaves are leathery and hang down vertically in most cases. The trunk is tall and straight, and grows at a remarkable pace. Saplings of the eucalyptus tree have been known to grow as much as 13 feet in a single year! In height, a eucalyptus can even challenge the giant sequoias of California. There are eucalyptus trees that are taller than 450 feet!

The eucalyptus is an extremely useful tree. It requires a great amount of moisture, so it is often planted in swampy regions. By drawing water out of mosquito infested swamps, it can actually help fight malaria in certain regions of the world.

One of the most remarkable things about this tree is that it actually provides man with a medicine. The leaves are dotted with pores that hold a straw-colored oil, which smells somewhat like camphor oil. This is eucalyptus oil. This oil is sometimes given to patients to be inhaled to clear the nasal passage.

Eucalyptus oil is also used as medicine internally. It has an effect on the kidneys, and it also depresses the nervous system so that it slows up breathing. It has even been used as an antiseptic by surgeons!

The wood of this tree is adaptable and durable. Eucalyptus wood is valuable in building docks and ships, and it is in great demand for the interiors of houses because it can be given an attractive, highly polished finish.

The words "perpetual motion" by themselves just mean motion that goes on forever. But usually when we say perpetual motion we are referring to a very special thing.

WHAT IS PERPETUAL MOTION?

For hundreds of years, men have had the dream of creating a machine that, once it is set in motion, would go on doing useful work without drawing on any external source of energy. Every machine now known has to have a source of energy.

A perpetual motion machine, however, would create its own energy in the form of motion. Every time a complete cycle of its operation was finished, it would give forth more energy than it had absorbed.

Most of the people who tried to create perpetual motion machines had practical purposes in mind. They thought it would be wonderful to have machines that could raise water or grind corn without the need of supplying any energy to the machine.

Is it possible to create a perpetual motion machine? Any scientist will tell you that the answer is no. The reason is based on what is one of the most important laws of science, the principle of the conservation of energy. According to this principle, energy cannot be created and cannot be destroyed in nature. Energy can be transferred from one place to another, energy can be freed or unlocked, but energy cannot be created. This means that any machine that does work must have a source of energy.

In the course of history, thousands of attempts have been made to create perpetual motion machines. The first attempts were made at a time when the law of the conservation of energy was still unknown. A great many others were simply fakes that were later exposed.

The antarctic region is the area around the South Pole. It includes the continent of Antarctica, which is the fifth largest continent. It is almost as large as the United States and Europe combined.

IS THERE ANY KIND OF LIFE IN THE ANTARCTIC?

This region is the coldest and bleakest part of the earth. It is surrounded by the world's roughest seas. It has strong winds, blizzards, little rainfall, and such severe cold that the whole region is almost useless. There is never enough sunlight to warm the land, and there is a year-round covering of snow.

The coldest temperature ever recorded in the world was in Antarctica, more than –100 degrees Fahrenheit. Because of the extreme cold, nothing seems to spoil, for there is no rot, rust, or bacteria.

What is to be found under the icy blanket of Antarctica? Not enough of it has been explored to really know. A few coal layers and small mineral veins have been seen by explorers. Probably other minerals do exist, but it would be so hard and expensive to get at them that they remain untouched.

ANTARCTICA

The only plants that exist there are the simplest forms—a few mosses, lichens, fungi, and algae—which are of no value and furnish no food. Only birds and animals that can find food in the sea live in the region.

The most common birds are skua gulls, snowy petrels, and several species of penguins. The penguins live and nest near the edge of the continent. They have underdeveloped wings and cannot fly on land, but in the water they are good swimmers. There are several kinds of seal in antarctic waters. The only industry in Antarctica is whale hunting. But so many whales have been caught there that there is now an international control to limit whale hunting.

Men have always identified themselves with animals or birds they admire. You have probably noticed how often the lion is used as a symbol by nations or in family crests.

WHY IS THE EAGLE THE NATIONAL EMBLEM OF THE UNITED STATES?

The eagle is such a majestic looking bird and gives such an impression of power in flight, that it has been used by man since ancient times as a symbol of might and courage. Did you know that as long as 5,000 years ago, the Sumerian people used the spread eagle as the emblem of their power?

In ancient Rome, the eagle was such an emblem too. The great emperor Charlemagne used the eagle as a symbol, and many German kingdoms later had it as an emblem. Even Napoleon adopted the eagle as his emblem of power!

So it is quite natural that when the new country, the United States, wanted an emblem, it turned to the eagle. Now it so happens that the eagle it chose, the bald eagle, is a bird found only in the United States and Canada. It is unknown in Europe.

In 1782, Congress chose the bald eagle as the emblem of the United States. On the national seal, the bird is shown with wings outstretched, holding an olive branch in one claw and arrows in he other. When the eagle is used in coins, military insignia and so on, it appears in many different poses.

By the way, it is called the bald eagle for a reason that may surprise you. It has nothing to do with hair. When the early colonists came to this country, this American eagle looked quite different from the gray eagle they had seen in Europe. The word "bald" originally meant "white," so they called this eagle "bald-headed," meaning it had a white head!

Every nation is proud of its Executive Mansion, or the home where its chief of state lives. In the United States, this is called the White House. Every year hundreds of thousands of people come to see it, or take a tour through certain parts of it.

WHO DESIGNED THE WHITE HOUSE?

Like any great building, the White House has a varied history. The cornerstone for it was laid in 1792, and it was completed in 1799. James Hoban, an Irish-born architect, designed the building. He based the design on certain buildings he knew and admired in Ireland.

The first residents of the White House were John and Abigail Adams in 1800, and since the house was quite new, the house was bleak and cold and not very comfortable. On August 24, 1814, during the War of 1812, the British burned the building, and only the walls were left standing. Hoban then rebuilt it, following his original design. The gray sandstone walls were painted white to cover the smoke stains. This, of course, explains the name it has—the White House. While this name was used for

South Side of the White House

the building for some time, it did not become official until the administration of Theodore Roosevelt.

The White House has been remodeled and altered many times, but the basic design remains. The main building is 170 feet wide and about 85 feet deep. Terraces extend from both sides of the main building. At the end of the east terrace is the three-story East Wing. There are offices here and this is where the public enters to tour the White House. Beyond the west terrace is the three-story Executive Office. This is where the president's office staff works.

Many of the upstairs rooms have been used for different purposes by different presidents, and their decoration has changed with the occupants.

HOW DID ANCIENT ASTRONOMERS PICTURE THE UNIVERSE?

It is much harder for us to understand the universe as we know it today, than it was for ancient man to grasp his idea of the universe. Today we consider the universe to include not only the earth and our solar system, but the galaxy to which this solar system belongs (called "the Milky Way"), and all the other galaxies as well. There are some 200,000,-000,000 stars in just our own galaxy—and there are millions of other galaxies stretching out into the universe. Man's imagination just cannot grasp this vastness!

But in ancient times, they had a very simple picture of the universe. They thought that the sun, moon, stars, and planets were small objects moving around the earth. They believed that the universe was as it appeared to them—with a vast, flat, immovable earth in the center and a great dome overhead, sprinkled with thousands of little shining lights.

The Greeks started the true science of astronomy. Most of the ancient Greeks thought that the earth stood still in the center of the universe. Pythagoras, who lived in the sixth century B.C., seems to have been the first to suggest that the earth is a sphere. But he still thought it was the center of the universe and did not move.

Aristarchus, who lived in the third century B.C., believed the earth was a sphere that rotated on its axis and revolved around a stationary sun. In the second century A.D., an astronomer named Ptolemy wrote a book called the *Almagest*. He thought the earth was the center of the universe, and he tried to show how the planets, the sun, and the moon moved around the earth. His ideas were accepted for 14 centuries!

Copernicus, in 1543, suggested the sun as the center of the universe. Then came the discovery of the telescope and man had a better means of finding out what the universe is really like. As more and more facts were gathered, our modern idea of the universe was gradually developed.

Suppose there were somebody in your town who cheated every time he sold you something. If you and your friends got together and decided not to buy from him anymore, you would be conducting a boycott!

WHAT IS A BOYCOTT?

The word "boycott" had a very interesting origin. In the days when many Irish landlords lived in England, their estates in Ireland were managed by land agents. It was the job of these agents to collect as much money as they could, regardless of whether or not the tenants could afford to pay.

One of these agents was Captain Charles Cunningham Boycott. In 1880, he refused to let the Irish tenant farmers decide how much rent they should pay and evicted them from their homes. As a result, the tenants chased away his servants, tore down his fences, and cut off his mail and his food supplies. Other tenants began to treat other land agents in the same way. When it happened to other land agents, it was said they had been "boycotted." Today it is applied to any organized refusal to trade or associate with a country, a business concern, or an individual.

When labor unions developed in the United States, they often used the boycott against employers. There were two kinds of boycotts. A primary boycott was when a body of workers refused to work for an employer or to buy his products. A secondary boycott was when these workers persuaded or forced other groups not to have any dealings with the employer.

In courts of law, the primary boycott has generally been held legal. But decisions by many courts have held the secondary boycott to be illegal because they affected the rights of third parties.

It is practically impossible to turn anywhere in our modern world and not see a form of art. Your furniture, your rug, the dishes in the kitchen, the car, your watch, even your clothes—all represent art in some form.

WHAT ARE THE FINE ARTS?

The reason is that somebody designed each thing, chose colors, and tried to make it attractive. But there is an important purpose behind this kind of art—and that purpose is to have things used. What we call "the fine arts" have a different purpose—and that is beauty.

The fine arts are considered to be painting, sculpture, literature, drama, music, dancing, and architecture. Of these, the only one which is also involved in "use" is architecture. Architects have to think about the usefulness of their buildings as well as about their beauty.

But in the fine arts, the end result of a lot of hard work by the artist may have absolutely no use at all. It was created to provide certain satisfactions we get from beauty, and that is all. So a statue, a tune, a picture, a play, a book, and a dance are all examples of the product of the fine arts.

Today, many curious experiments are being made in all the fine arts. But the traditional methods and products of the fine arts all have things in common. For one thing they have "design." Design can be with sounds, with stone, with words, with building materials, with lines, and paint. A work of fine art is designed. And within that design, the creator uses "rhythm," "balance," and "harmony."

Rhythm comes from the more or less regular repetition of similar sounds, colors, shapes, and movements. Balance is the arrangement of what the artist works with so that the result seems right to us. And harmony is putting things together that seem to belong together. These, of course, are only rough ideas of what a creator in the fine arts tries to do.

CHAPTER 2
HOW OTHER CREATURES LIVE

In the folklore and legends of countries all over the world, there are tales of great and horrible dragons.

They were pictured as huge, snakelike monsters frightful to behold.

| DID DRAGONS EVER EXIST? |

They had bulging eyes, their nostrils spouted flames, and their roar was so great they caused the earth to tremble.

One of the most famous of these ancient dragons was the Hydra, which had nine heads! It devoured many beautiful young girls before it was slain by Hercules. Another famous dragon was the Chimera, a fire-breathing monster that met its death at the hands of a young warrior, Bellerophon, who was helped by his winged steed, Pegasus.

Many dragons were supposed to be guarding great treasures. The Golden Fleece was guarded by a dragon with a hundred eyes! In other cases, great heroes always fought battles with dragons.

Although the dragon usually represents the spirit of evil, it has also been used as a symbol of protection. The early warriors painted fierce dragons on their shields to frighten away enemies.

People at one time actually did believe that dragons existed. For example, before the time of Columbus, sailors used to be afraid to venture into unknown seas because they believed huge dragons would swallow up the ships and men.

Of course, dragons never existed except in legends, myths, and fairy tales. Then why did the belief in them arise? In prehistoric times, all kinds of huge reptiles roamed the earth. The most terrifying of these beasts, the dinosaur, lived long before man appeared on the earth. But it is possible that during the time of the cavemen some reptiles of great size still survived, and from this came the legends of the dragons.

Scientists believe that dinosaurs first appeared on the earth about 180 million years ago, and died out about 60 million years ago. This is long before human beings appeared on earth, and also before such animals as

HOW DO WE KNOW WHAT DINOSAURS WERE LIKE?

dogs, rabbits, horses, monkeys, or elephants. Then how can we possibly know anything about these giant creatures?

Everything we know about dinosaurs—and everything we will ever know—comes from fossils. These are remains which these creatures left in the earth. But there are many different kinds of fossils.

The most common fossils are petrified remains of what were the hard parts of their bodies—bones, teeth, and claws. Scientists can study these remains and from them reconstruct how the whole body of the dinosaur was built!

Sometimes, petrified tendons and skin are found, and this provides even more clues. Fossils can also be trails or footprints that were made in wet sand or mud that hardened into stone over the ages. From these, it is

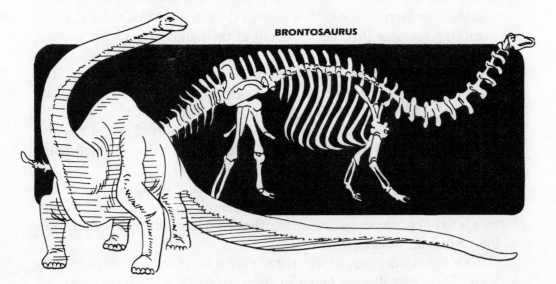

BRONTOSAURUS

possible to tell how the dinosaurs walked and whether it was on two legs or four. And the rarest fossils of all from this time are dinosaur eggs.

In this way we can tell that the Brontosaurus was a monster from 70 to 80 feet long and weighed about 38 tons. We know it lived in swamps and was a plant-eater. And we also know that a dinosaur called Allosaurus had sharp teeth and powerful claws and it fed upon Brontosaurus and other plant-eaters. You see, scientists have found, among the broken and deeply scratched bones of Brontosaurus—fossil teeth of the Allosaurus!

To begin with, there are many kinds of deserts. Some are the familiar deserts of bare rock and shifting sand, upon which the hot sun beats down. But some deserts, such as the Gobi, have bitterly cold winters. So a desert

HOW DO PLANTS AND ANIMALS LIVE IN THE DESERT?

is really a region where only special forms of life can exist. And the form of life is the kind that has adapted itself to the particular conditions of the particular desert.

For example, cacti are well-known desert plants. They have thick, fleshy stems without true leaves. Desert shrubs that have leaves usually have small ones. Little or no leaf surface prevents too much evaporation of water from the plant.

Many desert plants have thorns, spines, or a disagreeable taste or smell. This discourages animals that might eat them and so helps them survive. Desert plants usually lie dormant during the dry or cool season, or drop seeds that can survive such a period.

When the period for growth arrives, the seeds germinate and give rise to plants that rapidly flower and drop more seeds. Within a few weeks or months, the plants are ready again for the long season of dormancy.

When it comes to animals, they must be able to do without water for long periods, or be able to reach water holes at great distances. The camel, for example, is highly adapted to desert life. It has padded feet to walk on sand, a water-storing stomach, humps of fat as a reserve supply of energy, and nostrils that can be closed to keep out sand during windstorms.

Many of the smaller desert creatures need to drink no water at all. They get what liquid they need from the sap of food plants and from night dew on leaves or stones.

Long ago, voyages to distant lands were lengthy and dangerous undertakings. Travelers who dared make these trips brought back strange tales of the wonderful sights they had seen. Often they told of mythical animals,

WHAT WAS A UNICORN?

which were both strange and horrible. These tales grew more marvelous each time they were told.

Sailors told of seeing sea serpents, fearful man-eating creatures which were 200 feet long, 20 feet thick, and had bright blue eyes. Mermaids with long, green hair and shiny, scaly tails were supposed to haunt the seas and lure sailors to destruction.

Travelers said that in the countries they had visited they had seen unicorns. These were animals with the head and the body of a horse, the hind legs of an antelope, the tail of a lion, and the beard of a goat. Each unicorn had a single long, twisted horn set in the middle of its forehead. The horn was supposed to have the magic power to detect poison and was much sought after for drinking cups.

But the unicorn was a mythical animal that never existed, even though many people believed it did. Other mythical animals that people thought really existed included the griffins, animals that were a cross between a lion and an eagle. The Greeks told stories of centaurs, creatures which were half man and half horse. Almost everyone believed in dragons, huge winged serpents that breathed forth fire.

Although modern scientists have tried to explain what some of these mythical creatures really were, no one can explain where people got the idea that unicorns, centaurs, or griffins existed. A unicorn, by the way, is still on the coat of arms of England!

There is a very good reason why animals cannot learn to talk as human beings do, that is, use words to express ideas.

Most of the intelligent things animals do is a result of inheriting

WHY CAN'T ANIMALS LEARN TO TALK?

certain patterns of behavior. This works in special situations, but when you change the situation the animal usually does not know how to deal with it. The other reason animals behave "intelligently" is that they go through a trial-and-error method of learning.

Neither of these two ways of "thinking" can ever lead to talking. Talking means the use of words as symbols. The word stands for an idea or a thing—it is a symbol of it. And animals do not have the ability to deal with symbols. Their minds cannot use combinations of symbols the way human beings do.

The animal that most closely resembles man is the ape. Not only does the ape have a skeleton structure like man's, but he also has an "opposable" thumb. This means the thumb can be made to meet the finger tips,

WHICH ANIMAL RESEMBLES MAN THE MOST?

enabling the ape to use his hands to grasp things and to climb trees. Man's opposable thumb makes it possible for him to use tools.

Some people imagine that the ape is the ancestor of man, but this is not so. The theory of evolution holds that the apes and man may have had a common ancestor long ago, the so-called "missing link." But they evolved along different lines.

There are four kinds of "anthropoid," or "manlike" apes. The biggest and most powerful of these is the gorilla. Next in size is the orangutan. Then comes the chimpanzee. Finally, smallest of all is the gibbon.

The gibbon is the least known of the apes; he also resembles man the least. The gibbon can stand up straight on his hind legs and he can walk like a man instead of half-stooping. But the gibbon does very little walking because he spends most of his life in trees. He swings from branch to branch with his long arms, stopping to pick leaves and fruit.

When a gibbon eats, he is likely to sit erect like a man, even though his diet may include spiders, birds, and eggs. The family life of the gibbon is closely knit. His mate and their children stay with him night and day. And since a young gibbon will stay with the parents until about the age of six, a gibbon family may have as many as eight or nine members. In the wilds of the jungle, a gibbon may live to the ripe old age of thirty!

When an animal sheds its skin or feathers and replaces it, we call that "molting." Amphibians, reptiles, birds, and even insects molt.

Birds grow a whole series of feathers during their lifetime. When

WHAT IS MOLTING?

they reach the adult stage, they have the plumage that is typical of their kind of bird. Then adult birds change this plumage from time to time as old worn feathers molt (drop out) and new ones grow in their place.

If a feather is pulled out, it begins to replace itself at once. In addition, some birds grow bright, new feathers for the breeding season by molting. So most birds molt twice a year, once before and once after the breeding season.

Since most birds do not shed many of their flight feathers at the same time, they are able to fly all through the molting period. Also, flight feathers are often shed in pairs, one from the right and one from the left wing, so the flying balance is not upset. Ducks, swans, and geese are exceptions to this. They lose all their flight feathers when they molt, so they cannot fly. But since they are water birds they do not have to fly to escape from danger. They just take to the water.

During the molting season the brightly colored males often take on a drab-colored set of feathers. This gives them the protection of camouflage and makes it easier for them to hide.

Snakes have an interesting way of shedding their skin. A snake does not shed its entire skin, just the thin outermost part. The snake rubs its snout against something rough to loosen the old skin around the lips. Next it manages to get the loose parts caught on a rock or twig. Then the snake crawls out through the mouth opening of the old skin. It leaves the old skin in a single piece and wrong side out.

The chimpanzee is a monkey, but it is a special kind of monkey. It is the most intelligent one of all!

Monkeys belong to the highest order of mammals called "primates,"

IS THE CHIMPANZEE A MONKEY?

which includes man. All monkeys are covered with hair, usually live in trees, and have nails instead of claws on each of five fingers and toes.

Monkeys may be divided into four general groups: the lemurs; the Old World monkeys, including baboons, leaf monkeys, and others; the

New World monkeys, including the spiders, howlers, and others; and the apes, including the gorilla, orangutan, chimpanzee, and gibbon.

Of the three manlike apes, the orangutan, the chimpanzee, and the gorilla, the one that is most like man is the chimpanzee. This ape is smaller than either the gorilla or the orangutan, and it is more intelligent than either of the others.

The body of the chimpanzee, which has no tail, is similar to that of man, except that the chimpanzee has 13 pairs of ribs and man usually has only 12 pairs. Its flesh-colored skin is covered with coarse, black hair, except on the hands and face. As it grows older, gray hairs appear about the mouth and the skin becomes dusky or black.

Chimpanzees live in small bands in central African forests, from Sierra Leone eastward to Lake Victoria. They are captured quite easily, and live quite well in zoos. Sometimes they become so attached to favorite keepers in zoos that they will cry for them when sick!

Scientists who have studied them say there are at least 20 separate sounds that might be called a "chimpanzee language." On the ground they walk and run on all fours, and use their knuckles to support the weight of their trunk.

A male chimpanzee may weigh as much as 160 pounds and be about five feet tall, though most of them are somewhat smaller.

Dogs have been tamed by man longer than any other domestic animal. Hundreds of thousands of years ago, when giant, woolly mammoths still roamed the earth and men lived in caves, the dog first became man's friend.

WHY DO DOGS BURY BONES?

Despite the long history of being domesticated animals, the habits of dogs today can only be explained by going back to their ancestry before man tamed them. Strangely enough, scientists are not able to trace the origin of the dog as clearly as they can trace the history of the horse, for example. Some believe that dogs are the result of the mating of wolves and jackals a long time ago. Other scientists say that some dogs are descended from wolves, other dogs from jackals, others from coyotes, and some from foxes. The best theory seems to be that the wolf and our modern dog are descended from a very remote, common ancestor.

It so happens that many animals have instinctive habits today that are quite useless, but which their ancestors found necessary to life. These habits or instincts do not die out even though hundreds of thousands of years have passed. So if we recall that our dogs are descended from beasts which lived in a wild state a long time ago, we can explain some of their habits.

When a dog buries a bone today, it may be because his ancestors were not fed regularly by man, and had to store food away for future use. When a dog turns around three times before he settles down to sleep, it may be that he is doing it because his remote ancestors had to beat down a nest among the forest leaves or jungle grasses. When a dog bays, it is probably a reminder of the time when all dogs used to run in packs like wolves.

If you have a dog you love as a pet, you share some of your life with it. The dog lives in your home, keeps you company, and goes on trips with you. So it is hard to believe that the world this same dog sees is quite differ-

CAN DOGS SEE COLORS?

ent from yours. For dogs cannot see any colors.

Test after test has been made to find out if dogs can be made to respond to different colors in any way. Usually this has been done with food. One color would be a signal for food, the other colors were not. A dog was never able to distinguish colors from one another. Dogs probably rely on their remarkable sense of smell to tell things apart.

What about cats? The same kinds of tests were made. It was impossible to train a cat to come for its food in response to signals of different colors. It seemed that all the colors were like grey to a cat.

Is there any animal that is able to see colors? As far as tests so far have been able to prove, the only animal other than man that is able to distinguish colors is the monkey. Monkeys and apes have been trained to open a door which had a particular color in order to obtain food.

Actually, the color blindness of animals is quite understandable. Most wild animals hunt at night or graze in the evening when colors are dim. Most animals have coats that are rather dull-colored. Being able to see colors is not really that important to them in order to survive.

And most of them have developed their other senses such to the point where they can get along quite well in their own world.

When something tastes good, or you feel pleased about something, you might make a sound like "Mmmm—mm!" When a cat wants to express contentment, it purrs!

DO ALL CATS PURR?

The purring sound is caused by the vibration of the cat's vocal cords. When a cat takes air into its lungs, the air passes through the voice box that contains the vocal cords. If the cat then wants to express its satisfaction about something, it will allow the vocal cords to vibrate as the air passes in and out of the lungs during breathing. When it chooses not to purr, the passing air does not affect the vocal cords—and no purr!

Of course when we think of "cat," we usually mean only the domesticated cat. But there are many other members of the cat family. Did you know that the lion, tiger, leopard, cougar, jaguar, ocelot, and lynx are also members of the cat family?

When it comes to making sounds, our own domesticated cat not only purrs, it can also meow, howl, and scream. The other kinds of cats make different sounds. The lion and tiger can roar. The jaguar and leopard make a sound that is described as a hoarse cough or bark.

But an interesting thing about the lion, tiger, jaguar, and leopard is that because of a difference in the formation of certain bones in the throat, they cannot purr!

But all cats, large or small, have the same general proportions of the body. If you blew up a picture of a cat to a very large size, you would see that it looks very much like a tiger.

Three names for the same animal are: donkey, ass, burro. Then what is a jackass? It is simply the name for a male donkey. A female is called a "jennet."

ARE A DONKEY AND A JACKASS THE SAME?

The donkey is one of the oldest of domesticated animals. It was domesticated more than 5,000 years ago by the Egyptians.

Because it is such a useful animal to man, it has spread around the world, and there are many different kinds of donkeys. For example, the Somali wild ass, which is found in Somalia and other parts of Africa, is a shy animal that lives in groups of from 5 to 20. It eats the dry grass and shrubs of the desert. Some natives do not hunt it, but others hunt it for food, for its hide, or to export it alive. Today it is a rare animal.

There are wild asses that live in Asia. One type, the Syrian ass, once lived in Syria and other parts of the Middle East, but is now probably extinct. The ass is strictly a desert animal, and can go for some time without water. Just before the young are born they gather into great herds, but soon break up into small groups and scatter over the country.

The donkey of today is a descendant of the Nubian wild ass of northeastern Africa, where it once lived from the Nile to the Red Sea. Most of the wild types that existed in various parts of the world have been killed off. Today, man is trying to protect some of the few kinds that are left.

In many parts of Mexico and Central America, the ass, or burro, is a common means of transportation, instead of the horse or automobile.

There are many things about the opossum that make it a strange and interesting animal. To begin with, did you know that opossums belong to a group of animals called "marsupial"? The females of this group have

WHY DOES AN OPOSSUM HANG BY ITS TAIL?

pouches on the underside of the body in which the young develop. The kangaroos of Australia are probably the best known of this group.

Opossums are from 9 to 20 inches long with tails that are 9 to 13 inches long. Their fur is grayish white in color. Their round ears, long, narrow tails, and the palms of their feet are hairless.

The inside toe on the hind foot can be bent like a thumb to meet any of the other toes. The opossum uses his hind feet as hands. They help him climb trees. His long, flexible tail is also used in tree climbing.

Opossums spend a lot of time in trees, hunting and eating. Since they can use their hind feet like hands, they like to hang upside down when they eat. To do this, they wrap their tails around a branch, hang down, and grasp their food by all four feet. If they did not hang by the tail they could not use all four feet.

And what a variety of food they eat! Their diet includes small mammals, insects, small birds, eggs, poultry, lizards, crayfish, snails, fruit of all kinds, corn on the cob, mushrooms, and worms. At night, opossums invade orchards for fruit and hen houses for poultry and eggs.

The camel is called "the ship of the desert," and there is good reason for it. Just as a ship is constructed to deal with all the problems that arise from being in the water, so a camel is "constructed" to live and travel and survive in the desert.

WHY DOES THE CAMEL HAVE A HUMP?

Where other animals would die from lack of food and water, the camel gets along very nicely. It carries its food and water with it! For days before it starts on a journey, a camel does nothing but eat and drink. It eats so much that a hump of fat, maybe weighing as much as 100 pounds, rises on its back. So the camel's hump is a storage place for fat, which the camel's body will use up during the journey.

The camel also has little flask-shaped bags which line the walls of its stomach. This is where it stores water. With such provisions, a camel is able to travel several days between water holes without drinking, and for an even longer time with no nourishment except what it draws from the fat of its hump.

At the end of a long journey, the hump will have lost its firm shape and will flop to one side in flabby folds. The camel will then have to rest for a long time to recover its strength.

Did you know that the camel is one of man's oldest servants and has been used by man in Egypt for more than 3,000 years!

If you have never raised plants or flowers of your own, you probably thought of how delicate and harmless they are.

But there are at least three different plants that feed on insects, and

CAN PLANTS EAT INSECTS?

each one seems to be as clever and as cruel as any animal that goes hunting for its food.

The best known of these is the Pitcher plant, which grows in Borneo and tropical Asia. The Pitcher plant gives out a sweet juice that attracts insects. To make doubly sure of luring victims, this plant has a red-colored rim and cover. The insect comes over to take a look and to drink the nectar. It climbs over the rim of the plant, which is shaped like a pitcher. The inside of the pitcher is so smooth that the insect slides down and cannot stop itself. At the bottom, there is a bath of powerful liquid waiting for it. The insect is drowned and the liquid goes to work and digests the insect, thus providing food for the plant.

The Sundew is another tricky insect-eating plant. The upper part of each leaf is covered with little hairlike projections which give out a sticky fluid that attracts insects. This sticky fluid looks like dewdrops, which gives the plant its name. The moment an insect touches one of these hairs, it is stuck. Then all the other hairs start to bend toward the center of the leaf until they have wrapped up the insect in a neat package. The fluid that surrounds the poor victim starts digesting him. After about two days the job is done and the hairlike tentacles open up again.

In certain parts of North and South Carolina, we find a plant called Venus's-flytrap. This plant is the most business-like insect eater of all. It sits there with leaves spread open like hungry jaws. When a fly touches the hairs that grow along the leaf, the plant snaps it shut like a trap. After the fly is digested by juices in the plant, it opens up again.

Imagine yourself sitting or playing outdoors on a pleasant summer day. You hear a humming noise. Soon you feel a sting on your leg or arm. You slap hard. You look down and see a tiny speck of blood.

WHY WAS THE MOSQUITO MAN'S GREAT ENEMY?

You have just been engaged in a battle with one of the great enemies of mankind. To most of us, the mosquito is just an annoying pest. The humming noise about our heads (especially when we try to sleep) irritates us. The mosquito bite and the itching feeling afterward is a nuisance.

But this little insect is much more than a pest. The mosquito, by spreading such diseases as malaria and yellow fever, played a part in the fall of the ancient Greek and Roman civilizations. It killed many of our pioneer ancestors when they were opening our West. It prevented countries along tropical coasts and in hot climates from being settled and developing as they should. Fortunately, we have learned how to deal with the diseases that this "pest" used to spread throughout the world.

The male mosquito feeds only on plant juices, but the female prefers blood! So the female is the only one that bites you. And what equipment she has for doing an expert job of it! The "beak" of the female mosquito holds daggers with sawlike tips, plus a tube for injecting and a tube for sucking. As soon as she settles on your skin, she starts sawing. Into the tiny hole she injects a chemical so that your blood will not coagulate, or form a dry clot. Then she sucks up the blood she has prepared and flies off.

The itching you feel is not caused by the "bite." It is caused by the liquid she has injected. So if you kill her before she can suck back that irritating liquid, your itching will be worse!

Most of us think that spiders use silk only to spin a web. Actually, no other animal uses silk in as many ways as do spiders. They make it into houses, life lines, diving bells, cocoons, "airplanes," lassos, spring traps, and the web we all know.

HOW DO SPIDERS SPIN THEIR WEBS?

Spiders are not insects, but belong to a species called "arachnid." Unlike insects, they have eight legs, eight eyes in most cases, no wings, and only two parts to their bodies.

Spiders are found in practically every kind of climate. They can run on the ground, climb plants, run on water, and even live in water.

The spider manufactures its silk in certain glands found in the abdomen, or belly. At the tip of the abdomen there are spinning organs which contain many tiny holes. The silk is forced through these tiny holes. When the silk comes out it is a liquid. As soon as it comes in contact with the air, it becomes solid.

The spider makes many different kinds of silk. It makes a sticky kind that is used for the web, because this catches insects. For the spokes of the web it makes a stronger silk, which is not sticky. And it makes a still different kind of silk for the cocoon.

Even the webs that spiders spin are of many different kinds. The wheel-like web is the one we see most often. There are also "sheet" webs, which are flat and shaped like funnels or domes. And the trap-door spiders make a burrow out of their web with a lidlike opening at the top to catch and hold their prey. Other spiders build a bell-shaped home of silk which is entirely under water!

Everybody knows that birds migrate. This means that during certain seasons they travel over special routes. But few people realize that many butterflies, and some moths, also migrate.

DO BUTTERFLIES MIGRATE?

One example of this is the painted-lady butterfly. Each spring it travels from Mexico to California. In Europe, the same kind of butterfly crosses the Mediterranean Sea in spring, going from northern Africa to Europe. When there is a butterfly migration, thousands, and even millions, travel together across the sky.

The best known of all migrating butterflies is the monarch. It spends the winter along the Gulf of Mexico and other southern areas. In spring, the young female lays her eggs on the milkweed plants that have begun to grow. The caterpillars that hatch from the eggs feed on the milkweed leaves.

When the adult butterflies develop, they fly some distance north. There they mate and lay eggs on the milkweed that has just begun to grow with the advance of spring.

Now this is an interesting kind of migration. Because it means that within a few months time several generations of monarch butterflies travel farther and farther north in search of milkweed. By the time it is late summer and the monarch butterflies reach Canada, they are not the original ones that started out—but descendants of them!

When autumn approaches and cooler weather appears, those monarchs that have survived fly back in great numbers. They make a huge swarm of butterflies in the sky, and people have seen them spread out in a swarm 20 miles wide!

Such masses of butterflies migrate like this year after year, and they always follow the same routes.

The fly is an amazing and deadly creature. The fly spreads more death and suffering than an invading army. It does harm by spreading disease with its hairy feet and legs from the filth on which it feeds and in which it breeds.

HOW CAN A FLY WALK ON THE CEILING?

This little insect is wonderfully made. The house fly has two big brown eyes and each eye is made up of thousands of lenses. These two big eyes are called "compound eyes." The fly also has on top of the head, looking straight up, three "simple eyes" that can be seen only through a magnifying glass.

The feelers, or antennae, of the house fly are used as organs of smell, not of feeling. These antennae can detect odors at great distances. The mouth is made up of an organ that people call a tongue, but it is really all the mouth parts of an insect combined in one. This tongue is really a long tube through which the fly sucks juices.

The body of the house fly is divided into three parts: the head, the middle section, or thorax, and the abdomen. Behind the two transparent wings are two small knobs that help the fly balance itself in flight. The thorax is striped and has three pairs of legs attached to it. The legs are divided into five parts, of which the last is the foot.

The fly walks tiptoe on two claws that are attached to the underpart of the foot. Sticky pads under the claws allow the fly to walk upside down on the ceiling or anywhere else with the greatest of ease! It is because of these sticky pads and the hairs on the legs that the fly is such a carrier of disease germs.

Did you know that the entire life of a house fly is spent within a few hundred feet of the area where it was born?

There are thousands of different species, or kinds, of bees. So their habits and ways of life differ quite a bit. But probably the two things that we find most interesting about bees is how they produce honey, and how the "social" bees have organized their life.

WHAT HAPPENS TO BEES IN WINTER?

In producing honey, a bee visits flowers, drinks the nectar, and carries it home in its honey sac. This is a baglike enlargement of the digestive tract just in front of, but separate from, the bee's stomach. The sugars found in nectar undergo chemical changes while in the bee's honey sac as the first step in changing nectar into honey. Before nectar becomes honey, the honeybees remove a large part of the water by evaporation processes. Honey stored by bumblebees in cells called "honeypots" is almost as thin as nectar and will sour in a short time. Honey stored in the honeycombs by honeybees has so much water removed from the original nectar that it will keep almost forever.

What about the winter? In temperate regions, the young queen bumblebees pass the winter in holes they dig in well-drained sandbanks or in other suitable places. They are the only members of the colony that live through the winter! In the spring, each surviving queen starts a new colony.

The honeybees are luckier. They can adapt themselves to all extremes of climate. They have a social organization that is so efficient and complicated that it has been compared to that of man.

In the hive where they live, worker bees regulate the temperature with great exactness. They keep it at 93 degrees Fahrenheit where the young bees are being developed. During the winter, they do not let the colony temperature fall below 45 degrees. Honey stored in the hive is used as fuel by the bees. They have an efficient way of preventing the loss of more than a very small part of the heat they produce by consuming honey.

There is no other animal that man has fought with such energy for so long in so many places as the rat! There are many species of animals called rats, and most of them are harmless and interesting animals. But there

ARE RATS OF ANY USE TO MAN?

are two common rats, the black rat and the brown rat, that have caused all rats to be hated by man.

Why does man hate and fight the rat? Each year rats ruin hundreds of millions of dollars worth of grain. They destroy eggs, poultry, song birds, and spoil food in homes and on ships. Fires are caused by rats gnawing matches, gas pipes, and insulated electric wires. Houses may be flooded when they gnaw through water pipes. They damage floors and furnishings. Finally, they spread diseases such as the bubonic plague.

There are probably as many rats as people in the cities of the world. In the country, they actually outnumber human beings by three or four to one! They climb and burrow and live indoors or outdoors, in dry places or wet. Although they like vegetable food best, they will eat almost anything from dead animals and garbage to other rats.

And since they can live almost anywhere and increase so rapidly, they are hard to control. A female rat may have ten litters of young in a year, and the young are ready to produce more young in only four months!

**RAT IN SPACE SUIT FOR TESTS
IN SPACE CAPSULE**

But rats do have one important use to man. Since many of their organs work very much like man's, rats are used in laboratories for many experiments. New knowledge about diet, glands, and nervous reactions has been gained by experimenting on them. White rats, an albino variety of the brown rat, are used most often in tests.

If you have ever watched a snake move, there were probably two things about it that impressed you. The first, of course, was simply the mysterious ways in which a snake moves. You do not see any legs, the body

DO SNAKES HAVE BONES?

does not seem to have anything to push or pull it, and yet there it is moving! And the second thing is that the body seems to "flow" along the ground. It does not seem to have a bone in its body!

The fact is, however, that a snake is simply full of bones! A snake has a sectioned backbone, and to this backbone are attached pairs of ribs.

Some snakes have as many as 145 pairs of ribs attached to that very flexible backbone.

Ball-and-socket joints attach the sections of the backbone to one another, and each rib to a section of the backbone. So great freedom of movement of that backbone and the ribs is possible.

The tips of each pair of ribs are attached with muscles to one of the scales that are on the "stomach," or abdomen, of the snake. Because of this, a snake can move each one of these scales independently. When the snake moves one of these scales, that scale acts like a foot.

Snakes also have bones in their heads and jaws. A snake can open his jaws pretty wide when it is swallowing its dinner. This is because all the bones around the mouth and throat are loosely attached so the mouth can be stretched very wide. In fact, most snakes swallow their catch without trying to kill it first. Later on they digest it.

So you see snakes do have bones in their body, even though their slithery bodies look as if there's nothing solid in them!

Just because snakes do not have legs now, does not mean they did not have them at sometime in their development. But how and why they came to lose their legs is not known to science.

WHY DON'T SNAKES HAVE LEGS?

Some experts believe that the ancestors of snakes were certain kinds of burrowing lizards. There are many kinds of such lizards today, and all of them have very small legs or no legs at all. In time, the legs disappeared altogether. And despite this, snakes are able to move and get along very well indeed. One of the most helpful things for them in moving are the belly scales that cover the entire undersurface of most snakes.

There are four ways in which snakes move. One of them is called "lateral undulatory movement." In this method, the snake forms its body into a number of wavy, S-shaped curves. By pressing backward and outward against rough places on the ground, the snake slips forward on those scales.

A second way snakes move is called "rectilinear movement." In this case, small groups of the belly scales are pulled forward on part of the body, while other scales project backward to keep the snake from slipping back. Then the scales that have been holding the body are pulled forward. The scales that moved first hold the body.

A third way is a "concertina" method, which is used for climbing. The snake wraps its tail and rear part of the body around a tree, stretches out the forepart of its body and hooks it on the tree higher up. Then it releases the rear part and pulls the rest of its body upward.

"Sidewinding" is another method by which snakes move. A loop of the forebody is thrown to one side. Then the rear part is shifted to the new position, and another neck loop is thrown out.

All of us have seen pictures of "snake charmers" blowing on some musical instrument, while a snake rises up and seems to "dance" to the music. What is really happening?

CAN A SNAKE REALLY BE CHARMED?

The truth is that the "snake charmer" is not charming the snake at all! He is just putting on a show to make people believe that his music is making the snake perform. To begin with, snakes are deaf, so they cannot even hear the music he is playing! But snakes can pick up vibrations with great sensitivity. Even when they lie in a basket, if there are any vibrations in the ground near them, they notice them and respond.

What the snake charmer does, therefore, is to tap the basket or stamp on the ground, pretending he is merely keeping time to the music. The snake reacts to this vibration. The snake charmer also moves his body constantly, and the snake "dances" because of these movements the man makes. In fact, what the snake is doing is keeping its eyes fixed on the man, and as he moves it moves in order to keep him right before its eyes!

In Capistrano, California, there is a San Juan Mission. There are a great many cliff swallows there. For many years, newspapers have published stories about how these swallows return to Capistrano on March 19th, and not a day early or late.

DO SWALLOWS RETURN TO CAPISTRANO ON THE SAME DAY?

Now there are many birds all over the world that migrate and return each year to the same place. But no birds begin their migration on the same day each year, and no birds return on the same day each time. Many, however, do come fairly close to keeping such an exact schedule, which is why the stories arise.

The swallows of Capistrano leave the mission sometime near the date of October 23rd, but not always exactly on that day. And they return sometime near March 19th, but not necessarily just on that day. It is just a nice legend that people like to believe.

Swallows are interesting birds, even if they do not perform this migrating miracle. There are actually more than 100 species of swallows throughout the world. Cliff swallows are found in wild places and build their nests on the faces of exposed cliffs, or sometimes under the eaves of a house.

There are about 50 different kinds of birds of paradise, but they are all found in the tropical islands of the western Pacific and in northern Australia.

WHAT ARE BIRDS OF PARADISE?

Birds of paradise range in size from that of a crow to that of a sparrow, and each kind has its own special pattern of brilliant colors. It is this display of brilliant colors in their plumage that makes these birds so unusual. But these beautiful birds are actually related to the common crow.

The first Europeans to see these birds were the early Dutch explorers in the fifteenth century. They looked so beautiful that these men believed the birds were fed from the dews of heaven and the nectar of flowers, which explains their name.

Only the males have the brilliant plumage. The reason for this is not yet understood. It may be to attract the females, or it may be to draw natural enemies away from the nests of the mother and the young and so protect them.

Most birds of paradise build flimsy, platform-like nests in the treetops. In these they lay their streaked and spotted eggs. The birds eat almost anything they can find, from fruit to snails and insects.

During the mating season, the male birds gather and show off their fine feathers before the females. While these birds are usually wary, at this time they concentrate so much on showing off that hunters can shoot them at close range. The natives used to shoot them with blunt arrows so as not to injure the plumes.

There are a great many birds which can be taught to say a few words. But the real "talking birds" can be taught to say long sentences! The best talking birds are parrots, mynas, crows, ravens, jackdaws, and certain jays.

WHAT BIRDS CAN TALK BEST?

According to the experts the best bird talkers in the world are the African parrot and the myna bird of India.

Many people believe that the ability of a bird to "talk" depends on the structure of its tongue. A parrot, for instance, has a large, thick tongue. But many other talking birds have small tongues! Splitting a bird's tongue, which is done by some people to help it talk, actually has the opposite effect.

Do birds understand what they are saying? Most biologists believe birds do not understand the words they say, but they can sometimes form an association between certain expressions and actions.

The ability of certain birds to fly great distances and arrive "home," or at their destination, is one of the most remarkable things in nature. Do you know that carrier, or homing, pigeons were used to carry messages as long as 2,000 years ago by the an-

HOW DO PIGEONS FIND THEIR WAY HOME?

cient Romans? And even now, when modern armies have all kinds of wonderful equipment for transmitting messages, they still train homing pigeons for use in those situations when other methods of communication fail!

Many scientists have studied this amazing ability of birds, but no one yet has the full answer. One theory, which is better known than the others, is that pigeons use the sun to help them find direction. As you know, there is a different angle toward the sun as the day progresses—it is low in the morning, high at noon, and then low again. But some scientists believe a pigeon can see which path the sun will follow through the sky, and can figure out direction from this. It seems almost impossible to believe—but so far no one has offered a better explanation.

Not all birds or even all pigeons can do this. In fact, there are 289 different kinds of pigeons and doves, and they vary quite a bit. Some kinds of pigeons like to live and travel alone; others are always found in flocks. Some feed and live mainly on the ground. But most kinds live in forested areas and build their nests among the tree branches.

The electric eel is one of a group of electric fish. These fish capture their prey and defend themselves from enemies by discharging electric shocks. They closely resemble and are related to other fish, but they just

WHAT IS AN ELECTRIC EEL?

happen to have this electric power. Scientists still cannot explain the origin and development of the electric power in these fish.

The most dangerous of all the electric fish is the electric eel of South America, sometimes called "the Brazilian electric eel." This thick, blackish creature is an inhabitant of the rivers emptying into the Amazon and Orinoco rivers. It often grows to a length of six feet or more, and by a blow of its tail, in which its electric organs are located, it can stun an animal as large as a horse! Human beings are also said to feel the effects of the shock for several hours.

Another kind of electric fish is the electric catfish. This is sometimes four feet long and may be found in all the larger rivers of tropical Africa.

Third in the group of electric fish is the electric ray, or torpedo ray, found in all warm seas. It lives mostly in deep water near the shore. The member of this family inhabiting the Atlantic Ocean is said to grow to a length of five feet and weighs 200 pounds.

The electric ray is dark above and light below. It is round and flat and has a powerful tail. Its electric organs are situated between the head and gills. Experiments made on this fish have shown that its electric power can be used up and that the power will not return until the creature has rested and eaten.

Many people have had the experience of being at a public beach when the lifeguards ordered everyone out of the water because of the presence of jellyfish. It is hard to believe when you look at a jellyfish that this creature

ARE JELLYFISH DANGEROUS?

can be so dangerous.

Jellyfish are shaped like an overturned bowl. The digestive system is under the bowl. The digestive tract ends in a tube which hangs down from the center and has a mouth at the lower end. Tentacles, hanging from the edge of the bowl, gather food and are sometimes used for swimming. Between the tentacles are nerve centers and sense organs.

The bowl of the jellyfish is made up of two thin layers of tissue with jelly-like material between them. If a jellyfish is removed from the water

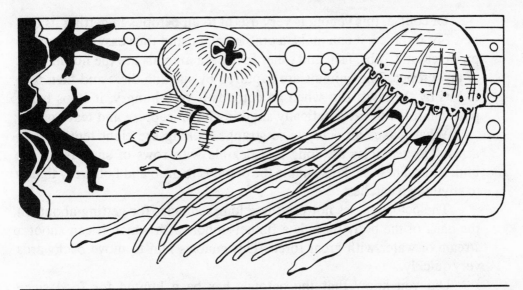

it dries up very quickly because 98 per cent of its body is water.

Of course, if the jellyfish is quite small, being stung by one may not be too dangerous. But when it comes to the big ones, that's a different story. Experts report that there are jellyfish with a bowl of over 12 feet in diameter and with tentacles more than 100 feet long!

When a jellyfish like this "embraces" you, it may make it hard for you to breathe and even partially paralyze you. The Portuguese man-of-war, which is one of the largest jellyfish, can kill and eat a full-sized mackerel. It can cause serious injury to human beings. There is a kind of jellyfish found off the coast of Australia called "the sea wasp," which has been known to cause death in many cases.

What makes the jellyfish dangerous are the tentacles. Some of them are barbed and pierce the body of its prey. The barbed cells are connected to poison glands which kill or paralyze the prey.

If you ever run into an octopus underwater, it might be a good idea to go off in another direction. Octopuses are not as dangerous as they look or are made out to be, but they can be very unpleasant.

WHAT DOES AN OCTOPUS EAT?

This is due to the bite of the octopus, which can be poisonous. An octopus has two very tough jaws that look like the beak of a parrot. Not only can the bite be painful, the octopus can inject venom or poison with its bite.

Of course, this venom is very useful to an octopus in getting its dinner. For instance, it can make a crab helpless, and thus easy for the octopus to eat it. Crabs, fish, and other living sea animals are the normal diet of an octopus. The animals are captured by sucking discs and then torn to bits by the jaws. But when an octopus is very hungry, it stops being particular. It will eat practically anything it can capture and tear apart!

What makes an octopus so strange looking are eight tentacles, or arms. The tentacles are long and flexible with rows of suckers on the underside. These suckers enable the octopus to grab and hold very tightly to anything it catches.

The octopus does not use these long tentacles for getting about. In the back of the body there is a funnel-siphon with which it can shoot a stream of water with great force. This enables him to move backwards very quickly.

Did you know that the octopus has been hunted for food since ancient Greek and Roman times? It was considered a great delicacy by the Romans. And even today, Greeks, Italians, and Chinese enjoy eating pickled or dry octopus.

Perhaps you have sometimes watched a snail moving slowly across the ground and wondered how it was able to move since no "legs" were showing. The fact is that the whole bottom part of a snail's body is

HOW DO SNAILS WALK?

really a "foot"! This foot is flat and smooth and contains muscles which the snail uses to glide along the ground. To help it move more easily, this foot has tiny glands which give out a slimy fluid, so the snail really glides over the surface with a wavelike movement.

Here's an amazing fact about this foot of the snail. It is so tough that a snail can crawl along the edge of the sharpest razor without hurting itself in the slightest! In fact, the snail is a remarkable creature in many ways. For instance, a snail never gets lost. It has an instinct that guides it back to its hiding place no matter how far away it has wandered. And even though a snail may weigh less than half an ounce, it can pull a weight behind it that weighs more than pound!

Snails are chiefly of two types, those with shells and those without. The snail that lives in a shell has a body that fits right into the coil of the shell, and it has strong muscles that enable it to pull its body entirely into the shell when there is danger. As an added protection when the body is in the shell, a horny disk at the end closes the opening tightly.

Snails live on land or in fresh water. Most snails eat plants of various kinds. The snail has a tongue that is like a file with hundreds of tiny teeth. It uses this to cut and shred its food.

A "fillet" is a thick slice of fish without the bone. So a "fillet of sole" should be a thick slice of a fish called "sole."

But the chances are that when you buy or order "fillet of sole" you

WHAT IS FILLET OF SOLE?

are really getting some other fish. The reason for this is that the sole is considered one of the most delicious fish in the world. In fact, many people consider it the best-tasting of all. But the fish they mean is the European sole—and not the American. The American sole is not a very good fish to eat at all. So when you buy or order "fillet of sole" in the United States, you do not get a "sole" but another kind of flatfish.

Among the more than 500 different kinds of flatfish are sole, flounder, fluke, halibut, and turbot. They have bodies that are flat like a pancake, and they lie and swim on one side with both of their eyes up on top.

But long, long ago, the flatfish did not travel and rest on their sides. They lived and moved in an upright position, and as a result they were being destroyed by their enemies. Then some of them, in order to survive, began to travel and rest entirely on their sides, and after thousands of years all flatfish began to do this.

But there was one problem. This meant that one eye would be buried in the mud and the mouth was at a bad angle for eating. So for thousands of years these fish began trying to twist the buried eye around to where it could see. And gradually this eye developed on the top of the head on the upper side!

The fantastic thing is that today, each flatfish after it is born goes through this process. It repeats the whole process of its evolution during its own lifetime—its eye actually travels across the top of its head and comes out on top!

A manatee looks like a small whale and it is a mammal, not a fish. The American manatee lives in the rivers of Florida, Mexico, Central America, and the West Indies. It measures from 9 to 13 feet in length. The body

WHAT IS A MANATEE?

is somewhat like a fish, but the tail is quite different. It is broad, shovel-like, horizontal, and has rounded edges. It has a thick skin which is hairless, except for "whiskers" on the upper lip.

Manatees live in bays, lagoons, and large rivers, but not in the open sea. As a rule, they prefer to stay in shallow water. When they are not feeding, they lie near the bottom. In deeper water, they often float about with the body arched, the rounded back close to the surface, and the head, limbs, and tail hanging down.

Manatees live on the plants they find in shallow waters. They use their flippers to push food to their mouths, and a manatee may eat 60 to 100 pounds of food a day! But then a grown manatee may weigh as much as 1,500 pounds. Because manatees browse like cows in the shallow waters and often are seen in small herds, they are sometimes called "sea cows."

Manatees usually give birth to one calf, but sometimes there are twins. To nurse the young, the mother rises to the water's surface and, with her head and shoulders out of the water, clasps the youngster to her breast with her flippers.

Manatees move very slowly and are perfectly harmless. But in some places today, manatees are still being hunted because of their flesh, their hide, and the oil which can be obtained from them.

Since a whale lives in the water and has a fish-shaped body, why isn't it considered a fish?

The fact is that the whale is a water mammal, and is descended from

WHY ARE WHALES CONSIDERED MAMMALS?

ancestors that lived on land. During the thousands and thousands of years they have been living in the water, whales have grown to resemble fish in their shape and other outside features, but they are built and they live like land animals.

A whale's flippers, for instance, have the bones of a five-fingered hand. Some whales even have the bones of hind legs in their flesh! The most important difference between whales and fish, of course, is that the baby whale is fed on its mother's milk like other little mammals. It is not hatched from an egg but is born alive. And for some time after it is born it stays close to its mother, who takes very good care of it.

Since all mammals have warm blood, and the whale has no fur coat to keep itself warm in the icy water, it has blubber instead. This is a layer of tissue under the skin filled with oil which retains heat and is as good as a fur coat!

Whales breathe differently than fish. Instead of gills, they have lungs and they take in air through two nostrils or "blow holes" on the top of their heads. When they go underwater, these nostrils are closed by little valves, so no water can get in. Every five to ten minutes, a whale rises to the top of the water to breathe. First it blows out the used air from its lungs with a loud noise. This makes the "spout" which we often see in the pictures of whales. Then it takes in fresh air and dives down into the sea to swim about.

The biggest whale also happens to be the largest animal in the world. It is the blue, or sulfur-bottom, whale, which may be more than 100 feet long and weigh 125 tons!

WHAT IS THE BIGGEST WHALE?

It may be found in all waters but is most common in the Pacific Ocean. It belongs to the group of whales known as "the whale-bone whales" (the other is known as "the toothed whales"). So whale-bone whales have no teeth.

It is rather strange to think that the largest animal in the world is able to get along without teeth! How do these whales manage? They have developed a structure in their mouths made up of hundreds of bony plates, known as a "baleen." It grows down from the palate (roof of the mouth) and forms a sort of sieve.

The whale feeds by swimming swiftly through a school of its prey—mostly small mollusks, crustaceans, and fish, with its mouth wide open. When it closes its mouth, the water is forced out between the plates, but the food is caught. The mouth of the whale is like a huge bucket. The head is about one-third the length of its body!

Of the toothed whales, the largest is the sperm whale. They may be 65 feet long and they have huge heads. The grampus, or killer whale (which is really a large dolphin), is the only one that eats other warm-blooded animals. It is about 30 feet long and easily catches seals. Packs of killer whales even attack large whales.

Because whales live in the water and have fish-shaped bodies, we tend to compare them with fish. But the skeleton, circulatory system, brain, and other organs are quite unlike those of fish.

Because the elephant is such a huge creature, it amuses us to think that a little mouse can frighten it. The reason many people believe a mouse can frighten an elephant is the idea that a mouse could get into the end of

ARE ELEPHANTS AFRAID OF MICE?

the elephant's trunk. They imagine this might suffocate the elephant.

The truth is, however, that elephants show absolutely no fear of mice! One can often see little mice running about in an elephant's stall, and the big beast seems to disregard them completely. And since the elephant has a very keen sense of smell, we cannot believe that it does not know the mouse is there.

Even if a mouse did have the courage to crawl into the opening of the elephant's trunk, the elephant could probably take a breath and blow it clear out of the cage!

Remember the trained seal at the circus who could answer questions in arithmetic by blowing on a horn? Or the horse who would tap his foot the right number of times when his trainer asks him to count?

CAN ANIMALS COUNT?

The truth is that these animals were not really counting! What happened was the seal or the horse would notice a sign from the trainer—it might be a movement of the head or lips or eyes—and this sign would tell him when to stop blowing the horn or tapping his foot.

Of course many animals can tell a larger quantity from a smaller quantity. For instance, many animals can pick a pile with six pieces of food instead of a pile with five pieces of food. Children who have not learned how to count yet can do the same thing. But being able to notice differences in quantity is not the same thing as counting.

Scientists now believe that certain birds and animals can actually count. In one experiment, a pigeon was offered one grain at a time. All the grains were good to eat, but the seventh grain was always stuck to the dish. After a while, the pigeon learned to count to six grains, and when the seventh grain was offered it refused to peck at it. This was real counting!

In another experiment, a chimpanzee was taught to pick up one, two, three, four, or five straws and hand over the exact number of straws that was asked for. But this was as far as this chimpanzee could count. It always made mistakes above five.

There are few animals that depend on flying for moving about as much as a bat does. While birds and insects fly too, they can manage to walk about if they have to. But the limbs and feet of a bat are not suited to walking.

WHY DO BATS HANG UPSIDE DOWN?

Which means they also can not stand easily. So when a bat is in its roost, the easiest thing for it to do is to hang on, head down!

The bat does a great many things that are quite remarkable. To begin with, the bat is a mammal—the only mammal that can fly. The young are born alive and feed on milk from the mother. When the young are very small, the mother may carry them with her when she goes hunting!

Bats are nocturnal, which means they are active during the night and sleep during the day. Since they have to hunt for their food, you would imagine that bats would need exceptionally good eyesight. But actually, bats do not depend on their eyes for getting about. When bats fly, they utter a series of very high pitched sounds. These sounds are too high to be heard by the human ear.

The echoes from these sounds are thrown back to the bat when it is in flight. The bat can tell whether the echo came from an obstacle nearby or far away, and can change its course in flight in time to avoid hitting the obstacle!

Most people think all bats behave more or less the same way, but since there are several hundred different kinds of bats, you can see why this is not so. There are bats with a six-*inch* wingspread—and bats with a six-*foot* wingspread!

People seem to think that goats will eat practically anything. And the truth is that's just what they do!

A goat's instincts will prevent it from eating things that will do it

WHAT DO GOATS EAT?

harm, but it will try to eat things most other animals reject. The reason for this seems to be that goats are rarely given the food and care bestowed on other domestic animals. The goat has been called the most optimistic of animals. Since it usually is not fed well, it will try to eat anything in the hope that it may be good.

The goat has always had a rather curious relationship with man. It is one of the most useful of animals. Since ancient times it has supplied man with healthful milk and satisfying meat. Its skin has been made into leather. Its wool has been woven into soft, warm cloth.

In spite of its usefulness, however, the goat has always had a bad reputation. This is probably due to its bad temper and the unpleasant odor of the males.

The goat contributes more to man in comparison to its size than any other animal. Goat's milk, for example, is considered by some to be better and healthier than cow's milk. It is often given to babies and invalids because it is easier to digest than cow's milk.

A few goats are raised for their flesh or are used as beasts of burden. Some are grown for their skins, which are made into goatskin, kidskin, and morocco leather. Other goats, such as the Angora and the Cashmere, are raised for their wool.

Goats were probably domesticated in Persia, but are now raised all over the world. There are about ten breeds of wild goats found in Europe, Africa, and Asia. They are sure-footed, active animals which usually prefer mountainous homes.

We think of ermine as a "royal" fur, and there is a reason for it. At one time in England, only members of the royal family were allowed to wear ermine. Later, nobles and government officials were allowed to wear this valuable fur. Their rank was shown by the arrangement of the black tail tips.

HOW DO WE GET ERMINE FROM A WEASEL?

Ermine comes from the weasel. It is the white winter coat that certain species of weasel develop. This happens to weasels only in cold regions, such as Canada, Lapland, and Siberia. Here the fur changes to pure white in winter. In milder climates, the fur changes only slightly from the summer coloring of reddish brown on the back and yellowish white on the underneath.

Weasels are closely related to skunks, minks, and martens. All of the species have slender bodies, short legs, sharp-clawed feet, and quite long necks. In the United States and Canada, the commonest species is the long-tailed weasel. The males are about 16 inches long and the females about 13 inches. Both have tails about four inches long.

The short-tailed weasel is about two inches shorter than the long-tailed species. It is also lighter in coloring, and the tail is only about two inches long. An even smaller weasel is found in Alaska and northern Canada. This is called a "least" weasel. There is a large species in the southern part of the United States that keeps the same coloring all year.

Generally speaking, the weasel can be considered a friend of man. Weasels are tireless hunters and they destroy vermin, rats, mice, rabbits, and certain birds. But many a farmer will tell you the weasel is quite an enemy too, because weasels love to rob poultry houses. A single weasel has been known to kill 40 hens in one night!

The guinea pig is not a pig, and it has nothing to do with Guinea. It is related to the hares and rabbits and its real name is "cavy." In other words, it is really a rodent.

WHAT ARE GUINEA PIGS?

Long before the Spaniards came to the new world, the Incas of Peru, Ecuador, and Colombia had domesticated this rodent. They used it for food, and considered it as a great delicacy. As a matter of fact, soon after the discovery of America the guinea pig was introduced into Europe for the same purpose, and was eaten by people everywhere. Nowadays, the only people who eat guinea pigs are some natives of Peru, but it is still kept as a pet by many people in South America.

A guinea pig is about ten inches long and weighs about two pounds. It has no tail. It has small, naked, rounded ears. The fore feet have four toes, the hind feet only three, and all the toes have broad claws.

They live wholly on vegetable food. While feeding they generally sit on their hind feet. When free they live in burrows and feed at dusk and on dark days. When they get plenty of green vegetation, they can get along without water. In captivity they may be kept on rabbit or rat food, but then they need water.

Guinea pigs have litters of two to eight or more, twice or three times a year. A few hours after they are born they can run about. Because they are gentle, easy to handle, and reproduce fairly quickly, they are very useful in laboratory experiments where live animals are needed. They have been very helpful to man in the development of medicines and medical treatment.

The very mention of the name "scorpion" makes us think of danger and poison. And the fact is that a scorpion can be a rather unpleasant creature to meet.

WHAT IS A SCORPION?

In the United States, scorpions have actually caused deaths in only one place—Arizona. The Arizona scorpion is related to the Durango scorpion that lives in Mexico. The Durango scorpion's bite can kill a man within an hour, and over a period of 35 years it has caused the deaths of about 1,600 people.

Scorpions are related to the spider. A scorpion has four pairs of walking legs and a pair of strong pincers which it uses to grasp its prey. It also has a long, thin, jointed tail which ends in a curved, pointed stinger.

This stinger is connected to poison glands.

When the scorpion walks, it carries its tail arched over its body. When it grasps its prey in its pincers, it bends its stinger over its head and plunges it into the victim. The poison will kill or paralyze the insects, spiders, and other creatures on which the scorpion feeds.

Scorpions are active mainly at night. During the day they hide in dark places, such as beneath a stone, in bark, or in dark corners of buildings. Adult scorpions always live and travel alone.

Young scorpions are born alive and cling to the mother's back. She does not feed them and after several days they go off on their own.

Scorpions are found mainly in warm climates. Of the roughly 500 species, 30 are found in the United States. Scorpions vary in size from half an inch to almost seven inches. The largest are found in the tropics.

Another name for the insects known as "aphids" is "plant lice." They are green or brownish in color, and the largest ones are not more than a quarter of an inch long.

WHAT IS AN APHID?

Aphids reproduce so rapidly that if they were not destroyed by their natural enemies, they would eat up nearly all the vegetation in the world!

Aphids may be found on the leaves, roots, and young stems of many kinds of plants. They often do serious damage to fruit trees, flowers, vegetables, and field crops. They have unusually strong mouths, or beaks, which stick out from their tiny heads. With these beaks they puncture the surface of the leaf and suck out its juices, thus causing the plant to wither and possibly die.

One of the most curious things about the aphids is that they serve as "ants' cows." Ants can actually "milk" them as if they were a sort of cow. What happens is that the aphids produce in their bodies a sweet liquid called "honeydew." Ants love to drink this liquid.

So ants capture these aphids and take care of them, just as a farmer might take care of his cows. The ants carry the aphid to the ant nest, supply it with plenty of green plants on which to feed, and protect it carefully from danger. When an ant wants to milk its cow, it strokes the aphid's sides gently with its long feelers. Then, as the tiny drops of honeydew flow from the rear of the aphid, the ant drinks the liquid!

Man, however, has no interest in protecting these insects, so plants are often sprayed with chemicals to kill them off.

CHAPTER 3
THE
HUMAN BODY

About 60 per cent of the human body is water! If you could squeeze out a human being like a lemon, you would obtain about 11 gallons of water.

This water, which is not like ordinary water because of the sub-

WHY DOES THE BODY NEED WATER?

stances it contains, is necessary to the life of the body. About a gallon of it is in the blood vessels and is kept circulating by the heart. This blood water bathes all the cells of the body in a constant stream. The water also acts as a conductor of heat through the body.

Even if you drink no water during a day, you take in about a quart of water from the solid foods you eat. So when you eat fruit, vegetables, bread, and meat, you are getting water because they are from 30 to 90 per cent water. In addition, the average person takes in about two quarts of water as fluids.

In the course of a day, about ten quarts of water pass back and forth inside the body between the various organs. For example, when you chew something and swallow it, you suck some saliva from the salivary glands and swallow it. In the next few moments, this water is replaced in the glands by water from the blood vessels. The swallowed water later goes from the stomach and intestine to the blood.

The amount of water in the blood always remains the same. Even though you may feel "dried out" after exercising on a hot day, the blood vessels contain the same amount of water. And no matter how much water you drink, it remains the same.

What happens to the extra water? It is stored away in various parts of the body. These include the intestine, the liver, the muscles, and the kidneys.

Most of us feel upset if we skip just one meal, and if we tried to go without food for 12 hours we would really be uncomfortable. But there are some people who seem able to "fast" for very long periods.

HOW LONG CAN MAN GO WITHOUT FOOD?

Various records are claimed for long fasts, but in most cases there is no medical proof and so the records are doubtful. One South African woman claimed that she went for 102 days living on nothing but water and soda water.

There are great differences among living things in the ability to survive without food. For example, a tick, which lives on animals, may survive a whole year. Warm-blooded animals use up their stores of food in the body more quickly.

In fact, the smaller and more active the animal, the more quickly it uses up its reserves. A small bird starves to death in about five days, a dog in about twenty. In general, we can say that a warm-blooded creature will die when it has lost about half its normal weight.

This matter of weight is important. Man and other creatures live in a state of "metabolic equilibrium," which means maintaining the body weight once a certain point has been reached. This regulation of body weight is done by thirst, hunger, and appetite.

When your blood lacks nutritional materials, this registers in the hunger center of the brain and you feel "hungry." The body is crying out for any kind of fuel (food). And it is our appetite that sees to it that we choose a mixed diet, which is the kind the body needs.

In order for the body to carry on its functions, it needs energy. This energy is obtained through the process of combustion. The fuel for the combustion is the food we take in.

WHY IS THE BODY WARM?

The result of this combustion in the body is not, of course, a fire or big heat. It is a mild, exactly regulated warmth. There are substances in the body whose job it is to combine oxygen with the fuel in an orderly, regulated way.

The body maintains an average temperature of 98.6 degrees Fahrenheit. It maintains this temperature regardless of what is going on outside. This is done by a center in the brain known as the temperature center, which really consists of three centers: a control center which regulates the temperature of the blood; one that raises the temperature of the blood when it drops; a third that cools the blood when the temperature is too high.

What happens if the blood temperature drops? Part of the nervous system is stimulated into action. Certain glands send out enzymes to increase oxidation in the muscles and liver, and the internal temperature rises. Also, the blood vessels of the skin contract, so that less heat is lost by radiation. Even the skin glands help by sending out a fatty substance that helps hold body heat in.

Shivering is automatically activated by the temperature of the blood dropping too low. The heating center of the brain makes you shiver in order to produce heat!

If the temperature of the blood rises, the cooling center goes to work. It dilates (opens up) the blood vessels of the skin so that the excessive heat can be eliminated by radiation, and perspiration can evaporate more easily. Perspiration is a quick method of cooling off for the body. When a liquid evaporates it takes heat from wherever it is located.

Every living creature must breathe in some way. All animal life breathes by taking in oxygen. Man gets his oxygen by taking air into the lungs.

It seems a simple thing for us to breathe. We do not even think about

HOW DO WE BREATHE?

it as we do it. But it involves quite a complicated process. When a person breathes in, air passes into the body through a series of tubes called "the upper respiratory tract." This starts with the nose. Here, particles which could be harmful to the lungs are stopped or strained out. The nose also warms the air.

From the nose the air turns down through the "pharynx," or throat. From here, the air goes through two smaller tubes called "bronchi," one of which enters each lung. The lungs are large, soft organs. Around the entire lung is a thin covering called "the pleura."

The lung tissue is like a fine sponge in some ways. But in the lung there are spaces, or air sacs, and it is here that air is received from the bronchi, the proper gases are used, and unwanted gases are forced out. These air spaces are called "alveoli."

The air we take in contains oxygen, nitrogen, carbon dioxide, and water vapor. These same gases are present in the blood but in different amounts. When a fresh breath is drawn in, there is more oxygen in the alveoli than in the blood. So the oxygen passes through the very thin walls of the blood vessels (capillaries) and into the blood. Carbon dioxide goes from the blood into the air sacs of the lung and is exhaled.

While there is much more to the process of breathing, of course, this is the most vital part of it—the exchange of gases that enables all the cells to obtain oxygen and to get rid of carbon dioxide.

An albino is a person without any color, or pigmentation. All races have a certain amount of pigmentation, though some among the white race (especially the Scandinavian) have very little.

WHAT IS AN ALBINO?

What causes color, or pigmentation, in people? It is produced by certain substances in the body acting on each other. The substances are color bases, or chromogens, and certain enzymes. When the enzymes act on the color bases, pigmentation is produced.

If an individual happens to lack either of these substances in his body, there is no pigmentation and he is what we call an "albino." The word comes from the Latin *albus,* meaning "white."

A person who is an albino has pink eyes, and this is because of the red of the blood circulating in the retina of the eye. An albino's eyes are very sensitive to light. So such a person keeps the eyelids partly closed and is constantly blinking.

The hair of an albino is white over his entire body. Even tissues inside the body, such as the brain and the spinal cord, are white.

By the way, albinism is found not only in man, but in plants and among all kinds of animals. It is even found among birds. And there is no race of man that may not have albinos.

It is believed that albinism may be inherited, and many people may not be albinos themselves but pass on the characteristics to their children.

Probably the albinos we are all most familiar with are white mice, rats, and rabbits. But there are people who have seen albino squirrels and even albino giraffes!

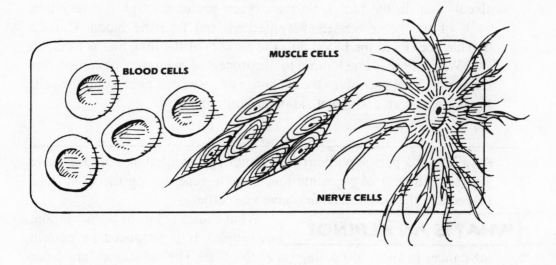

BLOOD CELLS

MUSCLE CELLS

NERVE CELLS

The cell is the building block that makes up living things. Everything that is alive is made of one or more cells. The simplest plants and animals consist of only one cell. Cells in more complicated living things work

WHAT DOES A CELL DO?

together. They are organized in groups, each of which has some special work to do for the plant or animal.

A tissue is a group of cells of a particular kind that does one particular type of work. For example, there is bone tissue, muscle tissue, or bark tissue. When tissues cooperate to perform a special task, such a group of tissues is called an "organ." An example of this is the human hand, which is composed of bone, muscle, nerve, and other tissues.

In the human body there are five important types of cells. Epithelial cells make up the skin and the glands and line the blood vessels. Muscle cells make up the three kinds of muscles. Nerve cells make up the brain, spinal cord, and nerves. Blood cells are found in the blood and lymph. Connective tissue cells make up the framework tissue of the body.

The circulatory system, in higher forms of living, carries food and oxygen to every cell and removes waste products, like carbon dioxide. The individual cells combine the food and oxygen slowly, thus obtaining the heat and energy necessary for their life and work. It is because of this energy that muscles can contract, nerves can conduct messages, and the brain can think.

The pituitary gland is part of the endocrine system of the body, so let us start with that. The endocrine system consists of glands located in various parts of the body. These glands produce active chemical substances called "hormones."

WHAT IS THE PITUITARY GLAND?

These glands send their secretions directly into the blood stream to be distributed throughout the body. The endocrine system as a whole is involved with "regulating" many things that happen in the body. And the pituitary gland, which is part of this system, controls many of the functions of the body. In fact, it is the most important part in the body in regulating growth, the production of milk, and in controlling all other endocrine glands.

A truly amazing thing about this vital gland is that it is about the size of a pea and weights about the same! It is joined to the undersurface of the brain and it is protected by a bony structure.

Even though the pituitary is such a small gland, it is divided into two distinct parts called "lobes"—the anterior lobe and the posterior lobe. And into the posterior lobe, which is the smaller of the two, go more than 50,000 nerve fibers connecting it with various parts of the body!

The pituitary gland controls growth in children by acting on another gland, the thyroid. The pituitary also controls the sexual development of a person. And it regulates the metabolism of the body, which has to do with the transforming of food into various forms of energy. It is also involved with certain muscles, the kidneys, and other organs.

Tumors that may grow on this gland can make it overactive or underactive. And one result of this activity can be to make people grow to giants or develop so poorly that they will be dwarfs.

Man has two sets of teeth: a first (primary), or baby set, and a second, or permanent set. In a full set of teeth there are four types, and each type has a special job.

HOW MANY SETS OF TEETH DO WE GROW?

The "incisors," in the center of the mouth, cut food. The "cuspids," on either side of the incisors, tear food. The "bicuspids," just back of the cuspids, tear and crush food. The "molars," in the back of the mouth, grind food.

There are 20 teeth in the first set, 10 in each jaw. They begin to form about 30 weeks before birth. In most children the first teeth to appear are the lower incisors. They usually appear when a child is about six months old. Between the sixth and thirtieth month, the rest of the primary teeth appear. The primary teeth in each jaw are the four incisors, two cuspids, and four molars.

Of the 32 teeth in the permanent set, 28 usually erupt between the sixth and fourteenth years. The other four, the third molars, or wisdom teeth, erupt between the seventeenth and twenty-first years.

The permanent teeth are four incisors, two cuspids, four bicuspids, and six molars in each jaw. The 12 permanent molars do not replace any of the primary teeth. As the jaws become longer, they grow behind the primary teeth. The bicuspids in the permanent set replace the molars in the first set.

The first molars, which are often called the six-year molars, usually are the first to erupt. They are the largest and among the most important teeth. Their position in the jaw helps determine the shape of the lower part of the face and the position of the other permanent teeth. They come in right behind the primary molars and often are mistakenly thought of as primary teeth.

The human bone is so strong it's a wonder it ever does break! Bone can carry a load 30 times greater than brick can. The strongest bone in the body, the shin bone, can support a load of 3,600 pounds!

HOW DOES A BROKEN BONE HEAL?

Yet as we all know, bone sometimes breaks as a result of violence. Each type of break has a name, depending on how the bone has been broken. If a bone is just cracked with part of the shaft broken and the remainder bent, it is called an "infraction." If there is a complete break it is called a "simple fracture." If the bone is broken into more than two pieces, it is a "comminute fracture." And if the pieces pierce the muscle and the skin, it is a "compound fracture."

Mending a broken bone is somewhat like mending a broken saucer. The fragments have to be brought into as close alignment as possible. But the big difference is that the doctor does not have to apply any glue. This is produced by connective tissue cells of the bone itself.

Bone tissue has an amazing ability to rebuild itself. When bone is broken, bone and soft tissues around the break are torn and injured. Some of the injured tissue dies. The whole area containing the bone ends and the soft tissue is bound together by clotted blood and lymph.

Just a few hours after the break, young connective tissue cells begin to appear in this clot as the first step in repairing the fracture. These cells multiply quickly and become filled with calcium. Within 72 to 96 hours after the break, this mass of cells forms a tissue which unites the ends of the bones!

More calcium is deposited in this newly formed tissue. And this calcium eventually helps form hard bone which develops into normal bone over a period of months.

A plaster cast is usually applied to the broken limb in order not to move the bone and keep the broken edges in perfect alignment.

You probably noticed that when you buy shoes and the man measures your feet, one foot is larger than the other. Since one foot does not do any more work than the other, why should this be so?

WHY IS ONE OF OUR FEET BIGGER THAN THE OTHER?

It is related to the fact that our body is "asymmetrical," that is, it does not consist of two identical halves, right and left. You can see this for yourself in many ways. If you look at your face in the mirror, you will notice that the right half of your face is more developed than the left. The right cheek is more prominent, and the mouth, eye, and ear are moulded with greater precision.

The same applies to the rest of our body. The legs are not equal in strength and dexterity. The heart is on the left side and the liver on the right, so that internally the body is not exactly balanced. The result is that our skeleton develops in a slightly unbalanced way.

Now this slight difference can have a tremendous effect on how we do things. The uneven structure of the body causes us to walk unevenly. The result is that when we cannot see, as in a snowstorm, a fog, or when blindfold, we will walk in a circle. The same is true of animals, whose body structure is also uneven. And if anyone were to drive a car blindfold, he would end up driving in a circle too!

When we come to the question of right-handed and left-handed people, we run into something curious. Ninety-six per cent of all people are right-handed. But this is not due to asymmetry of the body, it is due to asymmetry of the brain. The left half of the brain controls the right side of the body and vice versa. Since the left half of the brain predominates over the right half, this makes the right half of our body more skilled and makes most of us right-handed!

There are two main jobs that the skeleton does—it supports the body, and it protects delicate organs.

The skeleton is the frame that holds man erect. It is made mostly

WHY DO WE HAVE A SKELETON?

of bones. A baby is born with as many as 270 small, rather soft bones in his framework. A fully grown person usually has 206, because some bones become fused, or grow together.

Bones fit together at joints and are held fast by ligaments, which are like tough cords or straps. Some joints can be moved freely. For example, when you run, you move your legs at the hip and knee joints. When you throw a ball, you move your arm at the shoulder and elbow joints.

Some joints cannot be moved at all. At the base of the spine the bones are fused, forming one bony plate that fits into another. Neither moves. The joints in your skull are solid too, except for those in the jaw.

The protection that the skeleton provides includes the hard bony cap of the skull. This protects the brain. The rib cage protects the heart

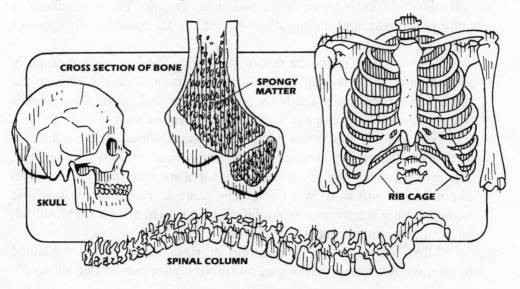

CROSS SECTION OF BONE

SPONGY MATTER

SKULL

RIB CAGE

SPINAL COLUMN

and lungs. And the backbone, or hollow spinal column, protects the spinal cord, the body's trunk line of nerve cables. The backbone is actually a string of small bones.

It is hard for us to think of bone as living tissue, but it is. It grows when a person is young. For example, the thigh bone may triple in length between the time a person is born and the time he is fully grown.

Bones grow in length and thickness as calcium and other minerals are added to them. And since bone is living tissue, it must be fed. The outside of the bone is covered with a thin, tough skin. The skin holds many tiny blood vessels that carry food to the bone cells.

The middle of a bone is spongy and filled with marrow. Some of the marrow is a storehouse for fat, and other marrow makes red blood cells.

Man is a mammal and all mammals have some hair. In the case of other creatures, we can see how having hair is useful. Its chief value is that it holds the heat of the body.

WHY DO HUMANS HAVE HAIR?

Hair protects tropical animals from direct sunlight. A long mane can protect an animal's neck. The hair of a porcupine helps it fight its enemies. But why do human beings have hair?

To begin with, an infant at birth is covered with a fine down. When a child is in the process of becoming an adult, this hair coat is transformed into an adult hair coat. And the development of this adult hair coat is regulated by certain glands containing special hormones.

In the male, these hormones cause hair to grow on the body and face, and hold back the growth of hair on the head. In the female, the hormones act in just the opposite way. There is less hair on the body and face, more hair growing on the head.

These differences in the male and female hair growth are what is called "secondary sex characteristics." That is, they are another way of setting the two sexes apart. The man's beard not only indicates he is a man, but is supposed to give the male an appearance of power and dignity.

Charles Darwin, a famous nineteenth century naturalist, believed that as man developed, he needed the fine hairs of the body to help drain off perspiration and rain water. The hairs that appear in certain parts of the body, such as the eyebrows, lashes, and the hairs in the ears and nose, help guard these body cavities against dust and insects.

The technical name for a birthmark is "nevus" and it refers to a mole which is present at birth or develops shortly after birth.

Medical science still does not know what causes them and no way has been discovered to prevent their appearance. But one thing is known: they are definitely not caused by some frightening experience the mother had before the birth of the child.

WHAT ARE BIRTHMARKS?

Almost everyone has at least one mole somewhere on the body. They can appear on almost any part of the skin, including the scalp. They may vary greatly in appearance since this depends on the layer of skin in which they originate. Most moles develop before or right after birth, but in some cases they do not show up until the child is about fourteen or fifteen.

If left alone, birthmarks rarely cause any serious physical problems. The greatest danger associated with them is the possibility that they may be transformed into a cancerous growth. But this happens very rarely and most people who have moles do not worry about this.

There is a whole variety of other skin disorders that might be considered birthmarks. One of these is a reddish or purplish structure or stain that appears on the skin at birth or shortly after. Sometimes these are strawberry or raspberry in color. They are actually an unusual formation of blood vessels, and usually disappear without treatment. But many doctors believe that strawberry or raspberry marks should be removed early in order to prevent leaving scars.

Medical authorities would even consider freckles to be "skin blemishes." They are caused by exposure to ultra-violet rays usually from the sun. People with blond hair and fair skins are the ones who most often get freckles.

Nobody likes to have pimples and blackheads, and it would be nice if we could say this is what causes them and this is how to avoid having them. But the problem is not so simple.

WHY DO WE GET PIMPLES?

Both pimples and blackheads start most often in the follicles of the hair. Certain glands, called "sebaceous glands," deposit an oily material there. When the hair follicle becomes plugged up and this deposit collects, it forms a blemish we call a blackhead.

Pimples are small raised areas of the skin which often have collections of pus in them. But the cause of pimples is harder to explain than that of blackheads. This is because they may be due to many conditions, including an improper diet, a glandular imbalance, or tiny infections in the skin.

Pimples may also be a sign that a more serious skin disorder is developing, or they may even be a sign of some diseased condition in the body. This is why a person should consult a doctor when he has many pimples on the body. The doctor will try to determine what brought them on. If the pimples are caused by some internal condition, then medication applied to the pimples will not do much good and could even damage the skin permanently. Pimples should not be squeezed. This makes it possible for bacteria to get into the area.

Acne is a condition that occurs in many young people of adolescent age. Acne includes blackheads, pustules, cysts, and nodules, all of which appear together. While the cause of common acne varies from person to person, in some cases it is due to the eating of certain foods, and in others it may be due to improper work by glands. A person with acne should consult a doctor for treatment.

About 10 to 12 per cent of all the people in Europe and America suffer from peptic ulcers at some time in their lives. What is an ulcer and what causes it?

WHAT CAUSES STOMACH ULCERS?

The gastric juice that is manufactured in the stomach contains hydrochloric acid, mucus, and an enzyme called "pepsin." Pepsin breaks down protein in the food into simpler substances.

Sometimes, however, the mixture of pepsin and acid acts on the wall of the digestic tract and the result is a peptic ulcer. These ulcers usually occur in the walls of the stomach.

People who develop such ulcers usually have a higher concentration of hydrochloric acid than is normal. There are other conditions that help in the formation of an ulcer, or hold back the healing process once one is formed. Tense, ambitious, hard-driving people are more likely to develop peptic ulcers than very calm people. Smoking may make an ulcer worse or delay healing of an ulcer. Coarse food also retards healing. But this disease may actually occur in any type of person at any age (though it is rare under the age of ten). Men get it four times as often as women.

How do you know if you have an ulcer? The pain tells you! The pain may occur from 30 to 60 minutes after eating. This pain rarely comes in the morning, but usually follows after lunch and dinner. And it may occur at night, after midnight.

The pain of a stomach ulcer is usually relieved by eating. When a patient has a peptic ulcer, the doctor puts him on a diet of soft foods with a lot of milk and cream, and orders him to rest and avoid fear and worry.

The appendix seems to be a part of the body that we can get along without, and even if it is healthy it does not do anything important for us. The appendix is a hollow tube, about three to six inches long, closed at

WHAT IS THE APPENDIX?

the end. In other words, it is a "blind" tube that does not go anywhere. It is found at the beginning of the large intestine in the lower right part of the abdomen.

So it is a kind of off-shoot of the large intestine. The wall of the appendix has the same layers as the wall of the intestine. The inner layer gives off a sticky mucus. Beneath it is a layer of lymphoid tissue. It is in this tissue that trouble may sometimes occur.

This tissue may become swollen when there is infection in the body. The contents of the intestine enter the appendix but are not easily forced out. If the tissue is swollen the contents of the tube may remain

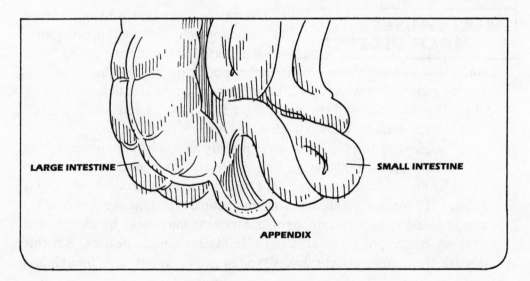

LARGE INTESTINE — — SMALL INTESTINE

APPENDIX

and become hard. The veins of the appendix may be easily squeezed by the hardened material and swollen tissue. This cuts off the blood flow and may cause infection.

Since appendicitis, or inflammation of the appendix, occurs very commonly, many people are constantly on the watch for symptoms. The typical symptoms are pain, tenderness, and spasm in the right side of the abdomen. Sometimes the pain is first felt in the pit of the stomach and then is concentrated on the right side.

In children, the first symptoms of appendicitis may be crying, vomiting, and refusing to eat. Sometimes parents give their children a laxative when this happens, and this is a very dangerous thing to do. A doctor should always be consulted at once when such symptoms appear.

There is only one treatment when a person has acute appendicitis: immediate operation to remove the appendix. It is a simple procedure and can be done quite safely.

You do not have to be an athlete to have athlete's foot. This is basically a fungus infection of the foot, and most persons are liable to catch it to some degree, though some people are especially sensitive to the

WHAT IS ATHLETE'S FOOT?

fungus. The name of this disease comes from the fact that it is often spread among athletes who share a common shower bath.

There are two chief types of athlete's foot. In the more common form, a crack appears in the skin, usually at the base of the fifth toe or between the fourth and fifth toes. There is also some loose dead skin clinging between the toes. When this loose skin is removed, the skin is red and shiny.

The second type of athlete's foot begins with a reddening of the skin between the toes, and it later becomes thick and begins to scale. Both these types may spread to cover part or all of the sole of the foot. And they may appear on both feet, though usually one foot is attacked more than the other.

There are several other diseases that can produce effects similar to athlete's foot. So a person who decides to treat himself with some medicine should be sure it really is athlete's foot. This is why it is safer to have a doctor examine your feet before you start your own treatment.

There are three types of fungi that cause athlete's foot. They are present on the skin at practically all times, so it is possible to get an infection any time. But when the skin becomes warm and remains moist for long periods, the fungi get into the dead outer layer of the skin and begin to grow. The fungi produce certain chemicals in the skin while they grow, and if a person is not allergic or sensitive to these chemicals he may not be bothered by the fungi at all.

Some mild cases of athlete's foot require no treatment and disappear as soon as the weather becomes cooler. But in more serious cases, the feet should be kept dry, socks should be changed frequently, and certain lotions may be helpful.

A stroke is a form of injury to the brain. Another name for it is "apoplexy."

When a stroke occurs, the flow of blood to a part of the brain is

| **WHAT IS A STROKE?** | suddenly cut off. As a result, all the structures connected with that part are |

injured.

There are several things that can cause this failure of the blood to reach parts of the brain. A blood vessel may be ruptured and cause a hemorrhage. A clot may form within a blood vessel. This is called "thrombosis." There may be spasm of an artery. Or a blood vessel may become closed off because of a small particle, usually a blood clot, floating in the blood stream. This is called an "embolus." An embolus is usually linked up with heart disease, but it may occur in other diseases too.

In terms of damage, it does not matter what cause the stroke. That part of the brain through which pass the nerves that control our voluntary motions, our sensations of pain, our temperature, touch, and vision may be damaged.

The most frequent cause of a stroke is thrombosis. Strangely enough, a person can have this kind of a stroke after a period of inactivity. For example, a person might wake up in the morning to discover that an arm, or a leg, or even a whole side of the body is useless. Or he may find that he can hardly speak or speak not at all. People with this kind of stroke have a pretty good chance for recovery, but there is usually some permanent disability.

In treating a stroke, the doctor has to find out what caused it, so he needs a complete history of the illness of the person. People who become crippled in some way by a stroke can often be rehabilitated, that is, trained to regain the use of the function that was crippled. This includes use of muscles and the ability to speak again.

The human body has 639 muscles, each with its own name! If all the muscles are put together, they make up the flesh of the body.

Most muscles are fastened firmly to the bones of the skeleton. The

WHY DO MUSCLES ACHE AFTER EXERCISE?

skeleton forms the framework, and the muscles move the parts of the body. Without them a person could not live. Not only would it be impossible to eat, breathe, and talk, but the heart would stop because its beating is a muscular action.

All muscle is made up of long, thin cells called "muscle fibers." But muscles differ in what they do and how they do it. They also differ in shape, appearance, size, and in other ways.

When a muscle contracts, it produces an acid known as lactic acid. This acid is like a "poison." The effect of this lactic acid is to make you tired, by making muscles feel tired. If the lactic acid is removed from a tired muscle, it stops feeling tired and can go right to work again!

But, of course, lactic acid is not removed normally when you exercise or work. In addition, various toxins are produced when muscles are active. They are carried by the blood through the body and they cause tiredness—not only in the muscle, but in the entire body, especially the brain.

So feeling tired after muscular exercise is really the result of a kind of internal "poisoning" that goes on in the body. But the body needs the feeling of tiredness so that it will want to rest. Because during rest, waste products are removed, the cells recuperate, nerve cells of the brain recharge their batteries, the joints of the body replace the supplies of lubricant they have used up, and so on. So while exercise is good for the body and the muscles, rest is just as important!

Anemia is a word used to describe many different conditions having to do with disorders of the blood. These conditions exist when the blood does not contain the normal number of red cells, or when the cells do not

WHAT IS ANEMIA?

have the normal amount of hemoglobin.

Anemia can be caused by poor blood formation, the destruction of cells, or by too much loss of blood. And these conditions, in turn, may be caused by many different body disorders. So when a doctor treats "anemia," he has to know exactly which type he's dealing with.

One kind of anemia, for example, can be caused by an injury that results in great loss of blood. Other body fluids seep into the blood to make up the volume, the blood is diluted, and the result may be anemia.

Another type of anemia is caused by an increased destruction of red blood cells, which can be the result of several conditions in the body. In some cases it may be inherited, or it may come from a transfusion of blood of the improper type, severe burns, allergies, or leukemia.

One kind of anemia many of us know about is nutritional anemia. The most common and least severe anemia of this kind develops when there is not enough iron for the formation of red cells. Iron is necessary for the body to manufacture hemoglobin.

Many of the common foods we eat contain only small amounts of iron. Also, many people cannot afford foods that have a high iron content, such as meat and leafy vegetables. So iron deficiency is not a rare condition.

The symptoms of this anemia are generally a paleness, weakness, a tendency to tire easily, faintness, and difficulty in breathing. If the patient is able to get enough rest and a good diet, he is usually able to recover quite rapidly.

In an adult human body there are about seven quarts of blood. These seven quarts form the most amazing transportation system imaginable.

The blood circulates through the body so that it reaches every one

HOW MUCH BLOOD IS IN OUR BODY?

of the billions of cells that make up the body tissues. It brings food and oxygen to each cell, carries away waste products, carries hormones and other chemical substances, helps the body fight infection, and helps regulate body heat.

The blood is made up largely of a colorless liquid called "plasma," and it is the red corpuscles floating in this liquid that give blood its red color.

It is when we consider how many of these blood cells there are in the seven quarts of blood that our imagination is staggered. There are about 25 billion of them! In a single drop of blood there are some 300,000,000 red corpuscles. If the cells were joined together in a chain, keeping their actual size, the chain would go four times around the earth.

Even though the cells are tiny, they have a tremendous surface area. For instance, if you could weave them into a carpet, the total surface area of this carpet would be 4,900 square yards. Since at any one given moment one-quarter of the blood is to be found in the lungs, about 1,200 square yards of blood-cell surface are constantly being exposed to the air. Every second, 2 billion blood cells pass by the air chambers of the lungs!

Because the air in lowland regions is under greater pressure, it contains more oxygen than at high altitudes. So the higher up a person lives, the higher is the number of blood cells he has. A person living in the mountain regions of Switzerland may have 50 per cent more blood cells than one living in New York.

What people call "heart attack" is one of the chief causes of death in the United States. In three out of four cases, the victim is a man, and the age is usually between fifty and seventy years.

WHAT IS A HEART ATTACK?

A typical heart attack is often caused by "coronary thrombosis." In fact, many people simply call it a "coronary." This is because it starts with the coronary arteries, the two blood vessels that supply the heart with blood.

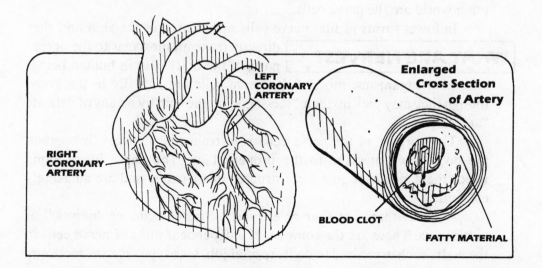

RIGHT CORONARY ARTERY

LEFT CORONARY ARTERY

Enlarged Cross Section of Artery

BLOOD CLOT

FATTY MATERIAL

When one of these arteries becomes clogged, the blood supply of part of the heart is shut off. The tissue in this part of the heart begins at once to degenerate and die, just the same as if it had been wounded.

When one coronary artery becomes clogged, the smaller branches of the other artery take up the work over a period of time. After a while, most of the areas of the heart that have been cut off receive the blood they need.

If the second artery can carry on the work for both, the person lives. Fortunately, in most cases the second artery can do the job, providing the heart is spared from all strain during this period.

In many patients, a heart attack occurs after some unusual physical exertion, emotional upset, exposure to extreme cold, eating a heavy meal —or any situation where the heart is called upon to do a bigger job than usual. These things do not actually cause the heart attack, but there is some relationship. In many cases, however, an attack can occur while a person is at rest.

The symptoms of a heart attack usually include pain beneath the breastbone. But the pain may also first be felt in the arms, neck, or left shoulder. There is sweating and shortness of breath. The person may become pale and be in a state of shock, and the pulse may become weak. A person should immediately call a doctor if such symptoms appear.

The cells whose job it is to keep our body informed of conditions in the outer world are the nerve cells.

In lower forms of life, nerve cells are located in the skin and they

WHAT ARE NERVES?

directly transmit messages to the deeper parts of the body. But in human beings and other organisms, most of the nerve cells are actually in the body, though they may pick up their "messages" in the skin by means of delicate "antennae."

The purpose of the nerve cells is to transmit messages throughout the body, each message to the proper place. The nerve fibers along which these messages go are constructed like a cable, and are amazingly efficient.

Actually there are four chief types of nerve cells, or "nerves," or nerve units. These are the completely independent units of nerve cells in the body, each organized to do its special job. One type receives messages such as heat, cold, light, and pain from the outer world, and conducts them to the interior of the body. These might be called "the sensory units."

Another type might be called "the motor unit." It receives impulses from the sensory units and responds to them by sending a nerve current to various structures in the body, such as the muscles and the glands. The reaction that results is called a "reflex." A "heat message," for example, would make certain muscles react and pull a hand away from a hot surface.

A third type of nerve unit does a connecting job. It transmits messages over longer distances in the body. It connects motor cells in one part of the body with sensory cells in another part.

A fourth type of nerve unit has the job of carrying messages from the outer world, such as cold, heat, and pain, to the brain where we "translate" the message into feeling.

There are very few cases of people walking in their sleep. But while sleepwalking is a peculiar form of behavior, there is nothing mysterious about it.

WHY DO PEOPLE WALK IN THEIR SLEEP?

To understand it let us start with sleep itself. We need to sleep so that our tired organs and tissues of the body will rest and be restored. We still do not have an exact scientific explanation of how and why we sleep, but it is believed that there is a "sleep center" in the brain which regulates the sleeping and waking of the body.

What regulates this sleep center? The blood. The activity of our body all day releases certain substances into the blood. One of these is calcium. It passes into the blood and stimulates the sleep center. And the sleep center has been "sensitized" before by special substances so that it will react to the calcium.

When the sleep center goes to work, it does two things. The first is it blocks off part of the brain so that we no longer have the will to do anything, and we no longer have consciousness. We might call this "brain sleep."

The second thing it does is block off certain nerves in the brain stem so that internal organs and our limbs fall asleep. Let us call this "body sleep." And normally these two reactions, or kinds of sleep, are connected. But under certain conditions they may be separated! The brain may sleep while the body is awake. This might happen to a person whose nervous system does not react normally. So such people might get out of bed while their brain is asleep and walk about! The brain and body sleep have become disassociated, and they are sleep walkers.

Did you know that you really cry all day long? Every time you blink your eye you are "crying"! You see, there is a tear gland that is situated over the outer corner of each eye. Every time your eyelid closes, it creates a

WHY DO ONIONS MAKE US CRY?

suction which takes out some fluid from the tear gland. This fluid we call "tears."

Normally, this fluid has only one purpose. This is to irrigate the cornea of the eye and so prevent it from drying out. But suppose some irritating substance reaches the eye? The eye automatically blinks and tears appear to wash the eye and protect it against the irritant.

We are all familiar with the experience of having smoke get in our eyes. It makes us cry. Well, the onion sends out an irritating substance too. The onion has an oil containing sulphur which not only gives it its sharp odor, but which irritates the eye. The eye reacts by blinking and by producing tears to wash away the irritant! It is as simple as that.

The onion is an interesting vegetable. It is a member of the lily family, and it is a native of Asia. The onion has been used as food for thousands of years, going back to the early history of man.

The three best known types of onion are the Spanish, the Bermuda, and the Egyptian. We actually import quite a lot of onions from Spain and Egypt, though we grow all kinds of onions right here in the United States. The Spanish and Bermuda onions are both mild in flavor, so they are usually the kind we try to eat raw. When you boil an onion you drive off its strong oil.

The simplest way to describe an optical illusion is that it is a "trick" that our eyes play on us. We seem to see something that isn't really so. Or we may be able to see the same object in two completely different ways.

WHAT IS AN OPTICAL ILLUSION?

If our eyes are functioning properly, and they are instruments for seeing exactly what is before us, how can they play "tricks" on us? Here is what makes it possible. Vision is not a physical

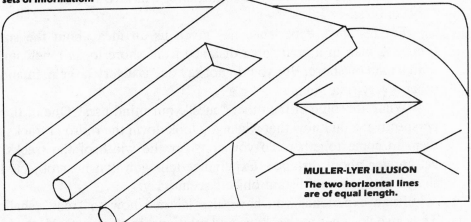

In drawing below, the eye wants to see a 3-D figure, but each end of the figure presents two separate sets of information. The figure makes no sense at all. Place finger across middle of drawing to separate the sets of information.

MULLER-LYER ILLUSION
The two horizontal lines are of equal length.

process. It is not like photography, for instance, which works mechanically. Vision is really a psychological experience, because it is not the eyes that see, but the brain!

The eyes are mechanical instruments for receiving impressions. But when those images reach the brain, a judgment takes place. The cells of the brain have to decide what they think this image is.

What helps the brain make that decision? One of the important things is the work that the eye muscles have to do in order to see a thing. In judging distances, angles, and the relationship of things in space, our eyes have to move back and forth. Our brain says that our eyes have traveled a certain distance because the brain has an idea of the amount of energy and the time it took for our eyes to move back and forth.

So now we have the possibility of one kind of optical illusion. Suppose there are two lines of equal length, but one is vertical and one is horizontal. The horizontal line will seem shorter to us because it is easier for the eyeballs to move from side to side than up and down. So the brain decides the horizontal line must be shorter!

When we look out across a field, how do we know one distant object is bigger than another, or that one is behind another? Why don't we see everything "flat," instead of in three dimensions, in proper relation to each other?

HOW DO WE SEE IN THREE DIMENSIONS?

The fact is that we "see" things not only with our eyes but with our minds as well. We see things in the light of experience. And unless our mind can use the cues it has learned to interpret what we see, we can become very confused.

For instance, experience has given us an idea about the size of things. A man in a boat some distance from shore looks much smaller than a man on shore. But you do not say one is a very large man and the other a very small man.

What are some of the other "cues" your mind uses? One of them is perspective. You know that when you look down the railroad tracks they seem to come together. So you consider the width of the tracks and get an idea about distance. Experience tells you that near objects look sharply defined and distant objects seem hazy.

From experience you have also learned how to "read" shadows. They give you cues to the shape and relationship of objects. Near objects often cover up parts of things that are farther away.

Moving the head will help you decide whether a tree or pole is farther away. Close one eye and move your head. The object farther away will seem to move with you, while nearer objects go the other way.

The combined action of both eyes working together also gives you important cues. As objects move nearer to you and you try to keep them in focus, your eyes converge and there is a strain on the eye muscles. This strain becomes a cue to distance.

Most people think we just have two tonsils, located on either side of the throat just behind the tongue. But this isn't true.

There are several pairs of tonsils of different sizes. Tonsils are small

WHAT DO OUR TONSILS DO?

bundles of a special kind of tissue called "lymphoid." Because of their location in the throat, they have a special job. They are the first line of defense against infections entering through the nose and mouth.

The largest pair near the palate are "the palatine" tonsils. High in the back of the throat are some smaller ones. These are called "the adenoids." Other small tonsils are found just below the surface in the back of the tongue, and there are still others in the back of the pharynx.

The tonsils are covered by the same smooth membrane that lines the mouth. In the tonsils, this membrane dips down to form deep, thin pockets called "crypts." The crypts trap germs and other harmful material from the mouth. The white blood cells surround the germs and help to destroy them. So fighting infection is the normal work of the tonsils.

Sometimes germs become active inside the tissue of the tonsils, and this may cause inflammation of the whole tonsil. This inflammation is called "tonsillitis." One or usually both palatine tonsils become enlarged, red, and sore. The crypts are swollen and sometimes discharge thick pus. This is acute tonsillitis. It is an infection that happens suddenly and usually goes away in four or five days.

Acute tonsillitis develops more often in childhood than in infancy or adulthood. It also happens more often during the winter months, when colds are common.

It seems like such a simple thing to us to sniff something and smell it. But the process of smelling, and the whole subject of odor, is quite a complicated thing.

WHAT IS SMELL?

Man's sense of smell is poorly developed compared to that of other creatures. Man's organ of smell is located in the nose, at least this is the place where the "messages" of smelling are received. This organ is quite small. Each side of the nose is only as large as a fingernail!

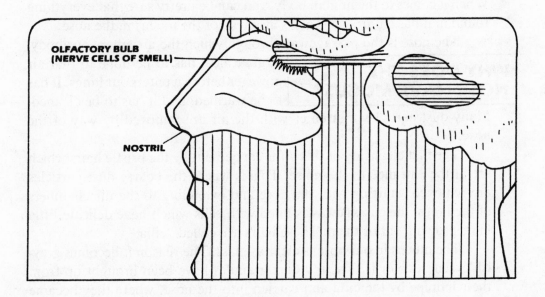

OLFACTORY BULB
(NERVE CELLS OF SMELL)

NOSTRIL

This organ is really a mucous membrane containing nerve cells which are surrounded by nerve fibers, kept moist by mucous glands. Through the cells, delicate hairs stick out into the nasal cavity.

But the tips of these hairs are covered by a fatty layer of cells. If they become uncovered and dry, our ability to smell disappears. In ordinary breathing, the stream of air does not come in contact with the smelling area, so if we want to smell, we have to sniff. This sends the air to the right place.

The substance that we smell must actually be dissolved in the fatty layer that covers the hairs before we can smell it! This is why it takes us a bit of time to "get" a smell. It is also why substances that have an odor have to be both volatile, or able to move, and part of an oily substance that can dissolve in that layer that covers the "smelling" hairs.

The way a thing smells depends on certain groups of atoms that carry odors. So that odor depends on a chemical formula, and each type of odor has a different chemical formula. And it takes only a very tiny amount of an odorous substance to excite our sense of smell.

There is a small smell center in the brain which receives the "messages" from the nerves in the nose and tells us what we are smelling.

When it comes to the human body, you can be pretty sure that everything found in it has a purpose. This is also true of the mucus in the nose.

The nose is the passageway through which the air enters our body.

WHY DOES THE NOSE HAVE MUCUS?

A great deal has to be done to that air however before it enters our lungs. It has to be warmed, and it has to be cleaned. Many dust particles that enter with the air are removed by way of the nose.

The first cleansing of this air is carried out by the bristle hairs which are at the entrance to the noise. This is where the coarse dust particles are removed. Starting with the nose and extending to the air chambers of the lungs, the passageway is lined with cells which have delicate little hairs growing out of them. These hairs are called "cilia."

The mucus in our nose is clear as glass. The reason it becomes greyish green in color is that tiny dust granules have been brought up from the windpipe by the cilia and carried into the nose, where they became mixed with the mucus.

Does "thought" take place at the fastest speed possible? In times past, this was held to be true, which explains the expression "quick as thought."

Today we know that thought is an impulse which must travel along a nerve fiber in our body, and this speed can be measured accurately. The surprising thing is that thought turns out to be a very slow process.

WHAT IS THE SPEED OF THOUGHT?

A nerve impulse moves at a speed of only about 155 miles an hour! This means that a message can be sent quicker outside of our body than from one part of our body to another! Television, radio, and the telephone all convey messages more swiftly than our nerves do. A thought traveling by nerve from New York to Chicago would arrive hours later than the same thought sent by telegraph, radio, telephone, or TV.

When something happens to our toe, for instance, it actually takes a while for that impulse to be received by our brain. Suppose you were a giant with your head in Alaska and your feet at the tip of South Africa. If a shark bit your toe on Monday morning, your brain would not know it until Wednesday night. And if you decided to pull your toe out of the water, it would take the rest of the week to send that thought back down to your foot!

Different kinds of "signals" make us react at different speeds. We react more quickly to sound than to light, to bright light than to dull light, to red than to white, and to something unpleasant than to something pleasant.

Everybody's nervous system sends thoughts at a slightly different speed. That is why certain people can react more quickly to signals than others.

How do we know what is going on in the world around us? We use our senses. Through them we can see, hear, feel, and taste.

But there are some scientists who believe that man can gain information without the use of senses. They believe the human mind has certain powers that have not yet been understood, and so it is possible to take in information that has not passed through the senses.

WHAT IS THE THEORY BEHIND ESP?

This process is called "extrasensory perception," or ESP. "Extrasensory" means "outside the senses." Many of the scientists who have studied this subject are psychologists. Their field of work is called "para-psychology." It is concerned with things that happen for which no physical cause can be found.

There are supposed to be three kinds of ESP. An example of one would be when someone seems able to read the thoughts in the mind of another person. A second kind of ESP is illustrated by this case: A woman living in one town dreams that her daughter, who lives in another town, had been hurt in an accident. The next day she learns that her daughter was hit by an automobile the night before.

A third kind of ESP would be the case of people who seem able to look into the future and know what will happen.

We know that some such cases really seem to happen, but many times it is difficult to really check the reports to see if they are true. Also, many people want to believe it and do not record very accurately what actually happened.

A great many experiments have been done by certain scientists to prove ESP exists, but the existence of ESP is still an open question for most scientists.

Sleep, as we know, is important to us because it helps restore tired organs and tissues in our body. But how much sleep do we actually need?

For most of us, eight hours seems to be about the right amount. Yet

HOW MUCH SLEEP DO WE NEED?

we know that there are a great many people who get along perfectly with less sleep, and some who may even need more. A great deal depends on the way we live. But a good general rule to follow is to sleep as long as we have to in order to feel happy and be able to work at our best when we awaken.

There are actually different kinds of sleep. There is a deep sleep and a shallow sleep. In a shallow sleep, our body does not get the same kind of rest it gets in a deep sleep, so that after eight hours of a shallow sleep we may still feel tired. But a short, deep sleep can be very restful.

Alexander the Great was able to get a deep sleep whenever he needed it. Once, during the night before an important battle, he remained awake longer than anyone else. Then he wrapped himself in a cloak and lay down on the earth. He slept so deeply that he did not hear the noise of the army preparing for battle. His general had to wake him three times to give the command to attack!

Normally when we go to sleep, our "sleep center" blocks off nerves so that both our brain and our body go to sleep. One prevents us from wanting to do anything, and the other makes our internal organs and limbs go to sleep. But sometimes only one goes to sleep and the other does not. A very tired soldier can sometimes fall asleep (brain sleep) and keep on marching, because his body is not asleep!

Just being able to stand up or to walk, is one of the most amazing tricks it is possible to learn! It is a trick, and it must learned.

If a four-legged visitor from another planet came to see us, he would

WHY CAN WE BALANCE OURSELVES ON TWO LEGS?

marvel at the ability we have to do this. If he tried to do it, it would take him a considerable time to learn the trick, just as it took time for you to learn it when you were a baby.

When you stand still, you are performing a constant act of balancing. You change from one leg to the other, you use pressure on your joints, and your muscles tell your body to go this way and that way.

Just to keep our balance as we stand still takes the work of about 300 muscles in our body! That is why we get tired when we stand. Our muscles are constantly at work. In fact, standing is work!

In walking, we not only use our balancing trick, but we also make use of two natural forces to help us. The first is air pressure. Our thigh bone fits into the socket of the hip joint so snugly that it forms a kind of vacuum. The air pressure on our legs helps keep it there securely. This air pressure also makes the leg hang from the body as if it had very little weight.

The second natural force we use in walking is the pull of the earth's gravity. After our muscles have raised our leg, the earth pulls it downward again, and keeps it swinging like a pendulum.

When you see an acrobat walking across a tightrope and balancing himself, remember he is only doing a more difficult trick of balancing than you do every day. And like you, he had to learn and practice it for a long, long time!

CHAPTER 4
HOW THINGS BEGAN

"Zoo" is short for "zoological garden." And a zoological garden is a place where living animals are kept and exhibited.

Why do we keep wild animals in zoos? The most important reason is

WHO STARTED THE FIRST ZOO?

that everyone is interested in animals. Another reason is that scientists are able to learn many important things by studying living animals.

The first zoo we know anything about was started as long ago as 1150 B.C. by a Chinese emperor, and it had many kinds of deer, birds, and fish in it. Even though it was somewhat like our modern zoos, there was one big catch to it. It probably was not open to the public but was kept for the amusement of the emperor and his court.

Since it costs a great deal of money to put together a zoo and maintain it, zoos in ancient times were assembled and owned by kings and rich lords. Many of them had collections of rare birds, fish, and animals of all kinds.

The first real public zoological garden in the world was opened in Paris in 1793. This was the famous Jardin des Plantes. In it were animals, a museum, and a botanical garden.

The next big zoological garden to be opened was in 1829 in Regent's Park in London. Then came the Zoological Garden of Berlin, which was begun in 1844 and became one of the finest and best in the world.

In the United States, the first zoo to be opened was in Philadelphia in 1874, and in the next year the Zoological Garden opened in Cincinnati. Today there are public zoos in most of the large cities in the United States and even in many of the smaller cities.

A duel, as we think of it today, is a prearranged encounter in accordance with certain rules between two persons with deadly weapons, for the purpose of deciding a point of honor. According to this definition, cer-

HOW DID DUELING ORIGINATE?

tain famous battles between two men were not really duels. For example, Hector and Achilles were supposed to have fought each other, but this was not a duel.

The reason for this is that in ancient times there was something called a "judicial duel." This was a legalized form of combat and it decided questions of justice rather than of personal honor. For instance, sometimes when a war was impending, a captive from the hostile tribe was armed and he fought with the national champion. The outcome of the duel was supposed to be an omen, since it was believed that the one who won deserved to win. At other times, such "duels" were a substitute for a trial in court.

In time, this form of dueling was abolished, and the duel of honor came into being. These began about the sixteenth century.

The custom of dueling became so popular that between 1601 and 1609, more than 2,000 Frenchmen of noble birth were killed in duels! The church and other officials protested against this custom, and in 1602 the French king issued an edict condemning to death whoever should give or accept a challenge to a duel or act as a second. This proved to be too strict, and in 1609 it was changed so that permission to engage in a duel could be obtained from the king.

Duels also became popular in England, and there too protests finally made them illegal. In Germany, however, student duels were a part of German student life until fairly recent times. It was considered an honor for a student to have participated in these duels.

Golf, as we know it today, probably originated in Scotland. But in tracing the beginnings of golf we have to go back hundreds of years before that.

In the early days of the Roman Empire, there was a game known as

WHERE DID GOLF ORIGINATE?

"paganica." It was played with a leather ball stuffed with feathers and a bent stick for a club. In England, there is evidence that a game like golf was played as far back as the middle of the fourteenth century. And in the British Museum there is a picture in a book from the sixteenth century which shows three players, each with a ball and club, putting at a hole in the ground.

During the fifteenth century, golf was becoming so popular in Scotland that laws were passed forbidding people to play because it was taking up too much of their time! Among other things, the interest in golf was causing people to neglect archery, and it was also interfering with attendance at church on Sundays.

Golf has been known since old times as the "royal and ancient" game. This is because royalty seemed to be very fond of it. James IV, James V, and Mary Stuart all enjoyed the game.

Golf clubs began to be founded in the eighteenth century. The first one was probably founded in 1744, The Honourable Company of Edinburgh Golfers. The Royal and Ancient Golf Club of St. Andrews, founded in 1754, frames and revises the rules of golf. Its decisions are accepted by clubs everywhere, except in the United States. In 1951, the Royal and Ancient and the U.S. Golf Association agreed upon a uniform code.

In the United States, golf was played as long ago as 1799. But another hundred years passed before golf began to be played in a regular and continuous way in the United States. The first golf club in the United States was founded in 1888 in Yonkers, New York.

All primitive people seem to have made music of some sort. But the sounds they made were very different from those of modern music. This music often consisted of long and loud exclamations, sighs, moans, and shouts. Dancing, clapping, and drumming went along with the singing.

WHO FIRST WROTE MUSIC?

Folk music has existed for centuries, passed from generation to generation by being heard, not by being written down.

Composed music is many centuries old. Ancient civilizations such as the Chinese, Hindu, Egyptian, Assyrian, and Hebrew all had music. Most of it was unlike ours. The Greeks made complicated music by putting tones together similar to present-day scales. For notation they used the letters of the alphabet written above the syllables of the words.

After the Greeks and Romans (who copied Greek music), the early Christian church was important in the growth of the art of music. Saint Ambrose and Saint Gregory began a style of music known as "plain song."

This was a type of chant sung in unison. Tones followed one another in a way similar to the method developed by the Greeks. Churchmen also learned to write music down. The modern method of writing music developed from their system.

In 1600, the first opera, *Eurydice*, was produced by Jacopo Peri. Later on, men like Monteverde wrote not only operas but music for instruments, such as the violin. Music began to be written for court dances, pageants, and miracle plays. And in time much of the great music we enjoy today was composed by such men as Bach, Handel, Haydn, Mozart, and Beethoven.

The first recording was made by Thomas Edison in 1877. His first machine had a cylinder turned by a hand crank. There was also a horn and a blunted needle, or "stylus." At the small end of the horn there was a flexible cover.

HOW WAS THE FIRST RECORDING MADE?

Sound waves that entered the large end of the horn moved this cover one way or another. To this the stylus was attached. It moved up and down with the sound waves too.

The cylinder was covered by a layer of tin foil. The stylus pressed against this foil. Gears moved the horn with its attached stylus slowly along the cylinder, as the crank was turned. In this way, as the stylus went around the cylinder many times, it made a crease in the tin foil.

When someone sang or talked into the horn, it made the stylus move up and down. The stylus made a deeper groove in the tin foil when it was down, a lighter crease when it was in an upward position. The changing depth of the groove was the pattern of the sound waves made by a person singing of talking. It was the record of the sound.

To play the record, the stylus and horn were moved back to the beginning of the groove. As the stylus followed the groove, it caused the flexible cover in the horn to vibrate in the same pattern. This made the air in the horn move to-and-fro, and this made a sound like the original sound recorded!

Man's desire to be able to take photographs goes back hundreds of years.

From the eleventh to the sixteenth century, there was a device called "the camera obscura," which was a forerunner of the photographic camera. Its purpose was to show on paper an image which could be traced by hand to give accurate drawings of natural scenes.

WHO MADE THE FIRST PHOTOGRAPH?

In 1802, two men, Wedgwood and Humphry, took an important step forward. They recorded by contact printing, on paper coated with silver nitrate or silver chloride, silhouettes and images of paintings made upon glass. But they could not make these prints permanent.

In 1816, Joseph Niepce made a photographic camera with which he could get a negative image. And in 1835, William Talbot was able to obtain permanent images. Talbot was the first to make positives from negatives, the first to make enlargements by photography, and the first to publish (in 1844) a book illustrated with photographs.

From then on, a whole series of improvements and developments came one after the other. The popular Kodak box camera was placed on the market in 1888, and photography as we know it was on its way.

Most photographic processes depend on the fact that the chemical silver nitrate reacts to light by turning black. And this was discovered way back in the seventeenth century by alchemists who were trying to find a way to turn common metals to gold.

WHO MADE THE FIRST PRINTING PRESS?

The first printing of any kind was done by the Chinese and Japanese in the fifth century. At that time and for hundreds of years afterward, books were so scarce and so hard to make, that few people could read or had books from which to learn.

The first printers used blocks of wood as the printing forms. Pictures were carved into their faces. The blocks were then inked and printed on the crude presses of the day. Later, words were added to the pictures, but these too had to be carefully carved into the wood.

A method was needed to shorten the long labor of hand carving each page. It took nearly a thousand years before any real change was made in the method used to reproduce the written word.

Many men were at work on the problem. Johann Gutenberg, a German printer living in Mainz, is generally believed to be the man who first

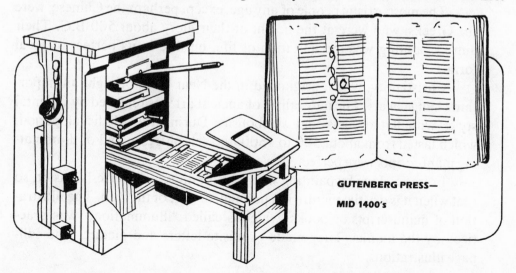

GUTENBERG PRESS—
MID 1400's

solved the problem. Gutenberg hit upon the idea of using movable metal type. He printed his first book, the famous Gutenberg Bible, by this method between 1453 and 1456.

Gutenberg's type was cast in a mold, each letter separately. When taken out of the mold, the type could be easily assembled, or "set," in words, lines, and pages. Once set and printed, the pages were broken up, and the letters reset and used again to print other pages.

This system is still in use today, though later inventors have greatly speeded up the ways in which the type is cast and set.

Many artists today paint pictures in which they make no effort to show the world around them. But when man began to paint pictures, that is exactly what he wanted to do. In caves, where early man lived thousands of years

WHO MADE THE FIRST PAINTINGS?

ago, paintings have been found that show animals as lifelike as can be.

These were made by the people of the Old Stone Age of Europe. Many thousands of years later, when the Egyptians had created one of man's first civilizations, paintings were also lifelike. The Egyptians believed there was a life after death, so they painted on the walls of their tombs everything that went on in their lives. There were figures of men, women, and children with animals, boats, and other objects.

The most artistic people of any age, except perhaps the Chinese, were the Greeks, who were at the height of their glory about 500 B.C. Their aim in painting was the imitation of life, but life in its perfect or ideal form.

Christianity, which originated in the Near East, brought an important change in art. The naturalism of ancient art was replaced by Oriental styles with flat designs and symbolism. During the Medieval period, which lasted from about 500 to 1500, the arts of fresco and of illuminating manuscripts were perfected.

Fresco is done by painting with a brush directly into fresh plaster, so that when it is dry the picture is a permanent part of the wall. The illustration of manuscripts or books, which is called "illumination," was practiced by the monks. They made exquisite letters and pictures and full-page illustrations.

A coin is a piece of metal of a given weight and alloy with the mark or stamp of those who issued it.

The first coins were made in the seventh century B.C. by the Lydians.

WHEN WERE THE FIRST COINS MADE?

They were a wealthy and powerful people living in Asia Minor. These primitive coins were made of "electrum," which is a natural composition of 75 per cent gold and 25 per cent silver. They were about the size and shape of a bean and were known as "staters" or "standards."

The Greeks saw these coins and appreciated the usefulness of a standard metal money, so they began to make coins too. About 100 years later, many cities on the mainland of Greece and Asia Minor, on the islands of the Aegean Sea and Sicily, and in southern Italy had coinages of their own. Gold coins were the most valuable. Next came silver and finally copper.

Greek coinage lasted for about 500 years. The Romans adopted the idea and carried it on for about another 500 years. Then the art of coinage declined. From the year 500 to about 1400, coins were thin and unattractive. But in the fifteenth century, the art of coinage was revived. Metal became more plentiful. Skilled artists were employed to engrave the dies.

The first coins in America were struck by the English in 1652. They were the New England shillings, and were crude coins about the size of a quarter.

Coins are issued by a mint, which is an institution established just for this purpose. It wasn't until 300 years after the discovery of America by Columbus that the United States Mint was founded.

WHAT WERE THE FIRST AMERICAN COINS?

Before that, coins were quite a problem in this country. During the long colonial period, there was a constant shortage of them, and those that were in circulation kept losing their value. There were a small number of English coins available, but they had to be used chiefly to pay for imports.

Some of the colonies tried to start their own mints, but the British government suppressed these movements. So most business was carried on by barter, which means the exchange of one product for another, or by the use of foreign coins that found their way into the colonies. The most popular of the foreign coins were the Spanish dollars.

After the signing of the Declaration of Independence, several of the states gave contracts to private mints to coin copper cents. Finally, in 1792, the United States Congress, using the right given to it under the Constitution, established the first mint at Philadelphia.

The act which established the mint provided for the coinage of the gold eagle ($10), half-eagle, and a quarter-eagle; the silver dollar, half-dollar, quarter-dollar, disme (later spelled dime), and half-disme; the copper cent and half-cent. The first coins struck in the new mint were silver half-dismes, made in October, 1792. According to tradition, these coins were made from George Washington's table silver, brought to the mint for melting from his home just two doors away! The first coins made for general circulation were cents and half-cents, issued early in 1793.

If you have never seen a goldfish before and had to think up a name for it, what do you think it would be? Perhaps you would look at its bright color in the sun and say it looks golden, so let's call it "goldfish"? Well,

HOW DID SOME FISH GET THEIR NAMES?

many fish got their names because of their appearance or some special quality about them.

For example, "shark" comes from the Greek *Karckarios* and the Latin *carcharus,* which mean "sharp teeth"! Does the porpoise resemble

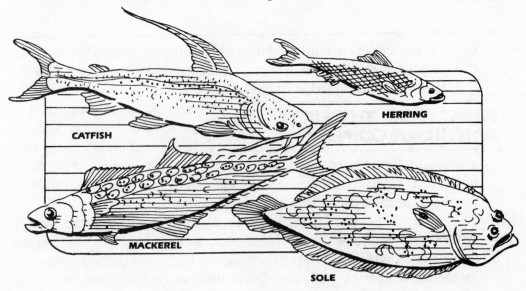

CATFISH

HERRING

MACKEREL

SOLE

a hog a little bit? It gets its name from the Latin words *porcus pisces,* which means "hog-fish." The swordfish is an easy one. The upper jaw of this fish really looks like a sword.

The whale is simply the modern spelling of an Anglo-Saxon word *hwal.* The sunfish is so named because it has a round shape like the sun. That catfish got its name because of its large, glaring eyes. Is there any question as to how the flying fish got its name?

The "sole" comes from the Latin word *solea,* which means "the bottom." Herring comes from an Anglo-Saxon word *haring,* which means "a multitude," or "many," and of course the herring is always found in multitudes.

Have you ever examined a mackerel? Then you probably noticed the spots on it. The word "mackerel" comes from the Danish word *mackreel* which means "spots"! A "smelt" got its name because it has a peculiar smell.

What's interesting about the salmon? The way it jumps over obstacles on its way upstream. So the word "salmon" comes from the Latin *salmo* which means a "leaping fish"! The trout loves to go after bait. And "trout" comes from the Latin *trocta,* which means "the greedy fish."

Nicknames often give a better description of the person or place we are talking about. This is also true of the states that make up the United States. The actual name of the state may have some historical basis, but the nickname gives us an idea of what the state and its people are like.

HOW DID THE STATES GET THEIR NICKNAMES?

Let's consider some of the most interesting ones and see how they started. Pennsylvania is called "The Keystone State" because it was the central state of the original thirteen and the seventh in order at the time of the formation of the Constitution.

Texas is called "The Lone Star State" on account of the single star in the center of its flag. Ohio is "The Buckeye State" from the number of buckeye trees that used to grow there.

Indiana is called "The Hoosier State" for a curious reason. In the early days, the boatmen of Indiana were quite tough and rude and they were able to silence anyone in an argument. So they were called "hushers," and in time this became "hoosier" and the name was applied to the whole state and its people.

Delaware is sometimes called "The Diamond State" because of its great value in proportion to its size. Michigan is called "The Wolverine State" because of the many prairie wolves that used to be found there.

Wisconsin is called "The Badger State," but not because badgers used to be plentiful there. The reason is that the first workers who came to the Wisconsin mines made homes for themselves in the earth as best they could, somewhat like the badger does, and these people came to be called "badgers." New York is called "The Empire State" because of its wealth and resources.

Honey is one of the most amazing products found in nature. It has been used since very ancient times, since it was practically the only way early man could get sugar.

WHEN WAS HONEY FIRST USED?

It was used by the ancients as a medicine, to make a beverage called "mead," and in a mixture with wine and other alcoholic drinks. In Egypt, it was used as an embalming material for their mummies. In ancient India, it was used to preserve fruit and in the making of cakes and other foods. Honey is mentioned in the Bible, in the Koran, and in the writings of many ancient Greeks. So you see its use goes far back in history.

There are hundreds of ways in which honey is used today. It gives flavor to foods, fruits, candies, and baked goods. It is used in ice cream. It is used in medicines and in feeding babies. It is given to athletes as a source of energy. Honey has antiseptic properties and has been used in healing wounds and cuts. It has been used in hand lotions, in cigarettes, in antifreeze, and even as the center for golf balls!

The cabbage is a very ancient plant, and the food plants that have descended from it include many that you would never imagine have anything to do with the cabbage!

WHERE DID THE CABBAGE COME FROM?

Thousands of years ago, the cabbage was a useless plant which grew along the seacoast in different parts of Europe. It had showy yellow flowers and frilled leaves. From this wild parent plant, more than 150 varieties of cultivated plants have been developed. The best known kinds are the common cabbage, kale, Brussels sprouts, cauliflower, broccoli, and kohlrabi.

In the common cabbage there is one central bud and the leaves grow close together about it, fold over it, and form a large, solid head. Red and white cabbages have smooth leaves. Fresh white cabbage is eaten raw in salads or cooked as a vegetable.

Kale resembles the wild cabbage, since all the leaves grow to full size and remain separate from one another. Brussels sprouts combine features of both cabbage and kale. Tiny cabbage-like heads form on the stalk at the bases of the larger leaves, which are full and open.

In the cauliflower, it is the delicately flavored flower buds and not the leaves which are eaten. These buds have developed into a solid mass with a few loose leaves around it. Because cauliflower was difficult to raise, the Italians developed a hardier variety called broccoli. Kohlrabi has a ball-shaped enlargement of the stem just above the ground, and these enlargements are eaten when young and tender.

Tradition gives the credit for designing the American flag to Betsy Ross. But historians doubt that this is quite accurate. We do know that in May, 1776, Congress appointed George Washington, Robert Morris,

WHY IS THE UNITED STATES FLAG RED, WHITE, AND BLUE?

and Col. George Ross to plan a flag. On June 14, 1777, Congress approved a design. But who actually suggested the design is not really known!

The idea of representing the 13 colonies by 13 stripes was used in the old flag of the Philadelphia Light Horse Troop, and this may be the origin of the stripes in our national flag. At one time, it was proposed that the Union Jack of England be kept in the upper canton, or corner. But then it was decided to substitute 13 stars for the Union Jack, and this is the resolution Congress approved on June 14, 1777: "Resolved, that the Flag of the United States be 13 stripes, alternate red and white; that the union be 13 stars, white on a blue field, representing a new constellation."

As new states joined the union, not only were new stars added to the flag, but new stripes as well! When the number of stripes had increased to 18, the shape was so bad that the original design had to be restored. Today, of course, we have 50 stars and 13 stripes on our flag.

While we cannot know how our flag happened to be red, white, and blue, we can take George Washington's interpretation of it as a noble one: "We take the stars from heaven, the red from our mother country, separating it by white stripes, thus showing that we have separated from her; and the white stripes shall go down to posterity representing liberty."

Piracy, which is robbery on the high seas, has been going on for thousands of years.

Even ancient Greek and Roman ships were often attacked by pirates in the Aegean and Mediterranean seas. In fact, the pirates became so powerful that they set up their own kingdom in part of what is now Turkey. The Romans had to send an expedition to destroy them in the year 67 B.C.

WHO WERE THE FIRST PIRATES?

A great period of piracy lasted from the 1300's to 1830. Pirates established themselves in ports of northern Africa in what were called the Barbary States: Morocco, Algiers, Tunis, and Tripoli. They would capture and loot European ships that sailed the Mediterranean and sell their passengers and crews into slavery or hold them for ransom. This piracy did not stop until the French conquered Algiers in 1830.

One of the names we have for pirates is "buccaneers." These were the pirates who operated during the late 1500's and 1600's in the Spanish Main. Originally the term "Spanish Main" meant the Caribbean coast of Central and South America. In buccaneering days it usually meant the Caribbean Sea itself.

The buccaneers were mostly sailors and runaway servants from different countries who had gathered on the islands and in the harbors of the West Indies. They hunted wild cattle and dried the meat over grills called "boucans," and that's how the buccaneers got their name.

Pirates often buried their gold, silver, and jewels in the ground. They wanted to keep their hiding places secret. There are many people who believe that a great deal of buried pirate treasure is still to be found along the Gulf Coast from Florida to Texas.

One of the oldest customs of mankind is the celebration of the New Year. How did it begin? Some people say the Chinese were the first to start it, others believe it was the ancient Germans, and still others claim it was the Romans.

WHY DO WE CELEBRATE THE NEW YEAR?

We know that the Chinese have always had a great festival at the time of their New Year which comes later than ours. The Chinese New Year festivals last several days.

The ancient Germans established a New Year festival because of the changing seasons. The German winter began about the middle of November. This was the time when they gathered the harvest. Because everybody came together at this time for the happy occasion, and because it meant they would have a period of rest from work afterwards, they would make merry and have a great holiday. Even though it was November, they considered it the beginning of a new year!

When the Romans conquered Europe, they changed this time of celebration to the first of January. For them, the coming of the New Year was a symbol of starting up a new life with new hope for the future. This custom and this meaning has lasted to this day. We greet the New Year happily, hoping it will bring us a good, new life!

The origin of many customs is hard to trace, but this one has a definite beginning . . . and it reads like a fairy tale!

Many years ago, a beautiful girl in Holland wanted to marry a

WHERE DID THE BRIDAL SHOWER GET ITS NAME?

miller. He did not have much money, but he was loved by everyone because he used to give his flour and bread to the poor.

The father of the girl objected to the marriage and said that he would not give his daughter her dowry if she married the miller. The people whom the miller had befriended heard about this and decided to do something. None of them had much money, but they thought that if each one contributed some gift, the beautiful girl and the poor miller could marry after all.

So they got together and went to the girl's house with their gifts. Some brought utensils for the kitchen, and others brought useful articles for the house such as linens and lamps. They "showered" her with gifts, and she was able to marry the man she loved after all!

This was the first bridal "shower," and the custom has remained ever since.

The wedding cake goes back to Roman times. In those days, among the highest members of the rich families, a special kind of cake was used in wedding ceremonies. The bride and groom not only ate this cake to-

WHEN DID THE WEDDING CAKE ORIGINATE?

gether, but treated the guests It is even said that the cake was broken over the bride's head as a symbol of plentifulness! Each of the guests took a piece of cake so they too could have plentifulness in their lives.

Many peoples all over the world have used bridal cakes in their marriage ceremonies. Several of the American Indian tribes had special kinds of cakes made, which the bride would present to the groom.

In Europe, it became the custom for guests to bring to the wedding spiced buns which were piled up in a big heap on a table. The bride and groom were supposed to try to kiss each other over this mound of cake for good luck. The story is told that a French cook, traveling through England, thought it would be a good idea to make one mass out of this mound of little cakes . . . and that is how our present kind of wedding cake was born!

Furniture is anything on which people sit, sleep, or eat. So when the early cave man slept on a wolf skin on the floor, that was his furniture. When he made a crude box in which to keep his bone tools, he made the first chest.

WHEN WAS FURNITURE FIRST USED?

The first records we have of furniture as we think of it today comes from the Egyptians. At least 4,000 years ago, they were using chairs, tables, stools, and chests. Some of the chairs had high backs and arms, decorated with carved animals' heads. Others were simple square stools with crossed legs which folded together like camp chairs. Egyptian beds were only a framework, often very low. The Egyptians did not use pillows. They used headrests of wood and ivory.

The Babylonians and Assyrians also had elaborate furniture. Kings and queens rested on high couches with footstools, or sat in high-backed chairs while they ate from high stands and tables.

Greek home life was very simple. The Greeks used only beds, chairs, and light tables for serving food. During meals the men rested on low beds and the women sat in chairs. The beds were like the Egyptian beds.

The Romans copied Greek styles. But they liked to fill their houses with objects for decorations, so they needed more kinds of furniture. They developed the cupboard, which they used for storing extra objects. They also used carved and painted wooden chests. The Romans made tables with metal, ivory, and stone decorations.

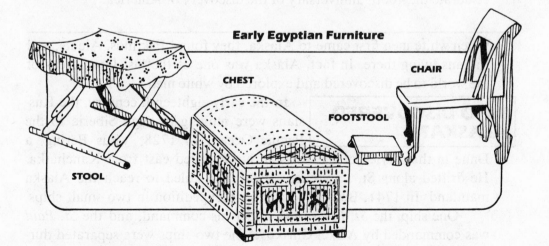

Early Egyptian Furniture

CHAIR

CHEST

FOOTSTOOL

STOOL

What we call a "world's fair" is really an exposition. The fair is one of the oldest and most popular means of selling and trading goods. Fairs are really large markets held in most parts of the world in important agricultural and industrial centers.

WHEN WAS THE FIRST WORLD'S FAIR?

Expositions, which are often called world's fairs, are for a different purpose. These large displays are set up mainly to show the industrial and artistic development of a particular country or a particular period.

The first exposition, or "world's fair," was The Great Exhibition of the Works of Industry of all Nations. It was held in Hyde Park, London, in 1851. The exhibition was housed in one building, the Crystal Palace. This permanent building was made entirely of iron and glass, like a huge greenhouse. It was destroyed by fire in 1936.

The first United States international exposition was in New York City in 1853. Although nearly 5,000 exhibitors took part, about half of them from 23 foreign nations, it was not a success.

The United States' first great exposition was the Centennial in Philadelphia, Pennsylvania, in 1876. It commemorated the 100th anniversary of the signing of the Declaration of Independence. There, for the first time, thousands of people saw the products and manufactures of the entire nation brought together. Alexander Graham Bell exhibited his telephone publicly for the first time at the Centennial.

After the success of this exposition, many others followed. Among them was the Columbia Exposition held in Chicago, Illinois, in 1893 to celebrate the 400th anniversary of the discovery of America.

When white men first came to Alaska, they found Eskimos, Aleuts, and Indians living there. In fact, Alaska was one of the last large areas of the world to be discovered and explored by white men.

WHO DISCOVERED ALASKA?

In the early eighteenth century, the Russians were moving through Siberia to the Pacific Ocean. In 1728, Vitus Bering, a Dane in the service of the Russian navy, sailed east from Kanchatka. He drifted along St. Lawrence Island, but failed to reach the Alaska mainland. In 1741, Bering led a second expedition in two small ships.

One ship, the *St. Peter*, was under his command, and the *St. Paul* was commanded by Alexei Chrikov. The two ships were separated during a storm, but both reached Alaska.

For the next 200 years, Russian fur traders hunted fur-bearing animals throughout Alaskan waters. They established many settlements, and in some of these places the quaint churches built by Aleuts and Indians under the guidance of Russian missionary priests can still be seen.

Later on, sea captains from Spain, France, and Great Britain explored the Alaska coast. But it was the Russians who used Alaska as a source of fur, and millions of these furs were sent by the Russians to European capitals. Then some of the fur-bearing animals began to be wiped out, and by the 1820's the Russians began to leave the Alaskan coast.

The Russian tsar, Alexander II, was not very interested in Alaska. William H. Seward, secretary of state under Abraham Lincoln, urged that we buy Alaska from the Russians. On March 30, 1867, the Alaskan territory was sold to the United States for $7,200,000. We bought it at less than two cents an acre! Today, Alaska is not only the 49th state in the United States, but its value to this country could hardly be measured in dollars!

If there is one sight in London that every visitor wants to see it is the Tower. The history and grandeur of England seems to be present wherever you turn.

WHEN WAS THE TOWER OF LONDON BUILT?

On the spot where the Tower now stands there was probably first a British fort, then a Roman one, and perhaps a Saxon one. William the Conqueror may have started building the White Tower, which is the oldest part of the present fortress. Most of the other buildings were put up during the reign of Henry III (1216-72).

William the Conquerer built the Tower in order to make the citizens of London afraid of him, but it has been used more as a prison than a fortress.

The Tower of London is still maintained as an arsenal. During the two World Wars, it was again used as a prison. It occupies a site on the old city wall of London and covers an area of nearly 13 acres. The outer wall is surrounded by a deep moat which was drained in 1843.

While there is a garrison of soldiers assigned to the Tower, the most interesting people tourists see there are the "Beefeaters." They are the "Yeomen Wardens," a body of about 40 men specially chosen for this job of defending the Tower. They wear a quaint costume which is said to date back to the time of Henry VIII or Edward VI. The reason they are known as "Beefeaters" is that in ancient times they were served beef every day as rations.

Tower of London

GUARD CALLED A "BEEFEATER"

Hawaii is the most recent state to become part of the United States. It is made up of a group of islands in the Pacific Ocean, some 2,400 miles southwest of California. The state includes eight large and many small islands, and has a total area of about 6,420 square miles.

HOW WAS HAWAII FORMED?

According to Hawaiian legends, there was a volcano goddess called Pele who formed the islands. From time to time Pele returns to the island's craters and kindles her fires into eruptions.

The strange fact is that the Hawaiian Islands are actually the tops of great volcanoes which have been thrust up from the bottom of the ocean. For example, the island of Hawaii ("the Big Island"), which is twice as large as all the other islands together, was piled up by five volcanoes whose eruptions overlapped one another. Two of these are still active and they are still continuing the process of island building.

One of these volcanoes, Mauna Loa, erupts every few years. In 1950, it erupted for 23 days and lava flowed down into the sea. It turned the water into steam, killing many fish.

Another volcano, Mauna Kea, is dormant. It is the highest mountain in the Pacific. It rises over 13,780 feet above sea level, but its base goes down to about 18,000 feet under the ocean. If measured from its underwater base, it is the world's tallest mountain.

On the island of Maui there is a volcano called Haleakala which rises to a height of about 10,025 feet. It is the world's largest inactive volcano. Its crater is about 20 miles around and some 2,720 feet deep.

The word "college" originally meant any society or union of persons engaged in some common activity. For example, there is a college of cardinals which elects the pope at Rome, and the United States has an

WHEN WAS THE FIRST UNIVERSITY STARTED?

electoral college to choose the president and vice president.

In medieval times, any corporation or society organized for a common interest was called a "university." So the earliest educational universities were merely societies of scholars or teachers formed for mutual protection. There were no permanent buildings. Instructors and students simply rented a hall or a large room.

In time, these institutions grew, buildings were built, certain legal rights and privileges were obtained, and the universities became permanent. The first such university was in Salerno, Italy. As far back as the ninth century it was well known as a school of medicine. It was formally made a university in 1231.

Toward the end of the twelfth century at Bologna, Italy, a many-sided university was established, The school at Bologna taught law, medicine, arts, and theology.

The most famous of the medieval schools of higher learning was the University of Paris, officially organized in the last half of the twelfth century. It became a model for all the later universities of Europe.

Two great English universities were modeled upon the University of Paris. Oxford and Cambridge were both legally recognized by the thirteenth century. A university, remember, usually includes a number of colleges. This means that degrees are given in many different fields at a university.

Many institutions start as colleges and later become universities. In the United States, the first college was Harvard, founded at Cambridge, Massachusetts, in 1636. Today it is a great university.

Men have lived together in groups since the very earliest times. Each group tried to keep together and to find ways that would keep the group going after its individual members were gone.

WHY WERE SCHOOLS STARTED?

In order for the group and its values to survive, it was necessary for the older members to teach children all that they had learned so that they could solve the problems they would face. Young people had to be trained to carry on the customs, knowledge, and skills of the group. So the idea of "education" existed long before there were actual schools.

But when letters were invented, schools became a necessity. Special learning was required to master the symbols. And the existence of these symbols made it possible to accumulate and transmit knowledge on a scale that had never been possible before.

Ordinary life in the group did not provide this type of education. So a special organization was needed to take over the job of providing it. And this was the school.

Nobody knows when the first schools appeared. We do know that they were in existence in Egypt and perhaps in China and in some other countries 5,000 to 6,000 years ago.

Actually, it was not until the eighteenth century that the idea of education for all as a way of improving man and his society began to spread. And it was only about 100 years ago that people began to consider an education as the right of every child.

The principal religions in the world today are the Hindu, Buddhist, Confucianist, Taoist, Shinto, Zoroastrian, Mohammedan, Jewish, and Christian.

HOW DID THE MAJOR RELIGIONS START?

The Hindu religion of India was formed about 3,000 years ago. Founders of this faith considered that Brahma was the first great god. Brahma created all forms of life and multiples of other gods.

Buddha was a great religious teacher who lived about 3,000 years ago. In its original form Buddhism does not depend upon a god or gods but teaches that man can purify himself of all desires and thus do away with evil and suffering. There are various sects and modifications of Buddhism.

Confucianism, based on the teachings of Confucius, a sixth century B.C. philosopher, is concerned almost wholly with man's right conduct toward his fellow man.

Taoism sprang from a little book called *Tao Te king,* which was written by Lâo-tse in the sixth century B.C. It calls upon its followers to find and follow the natural way of life.

Shinto is the primitive religion of Japan. It has been modified by many later contacts and teachers, mostly Chinese.

The Zoroastrian religion stems from the teachings of Zarathustra, or Zoroaster, prophet of Iran born probably in the seventh century B.C. This religion elevates Ahura Mazda (Wise Lord) as the great One God. The Mohammedan religion is based on the teachings of Mohammed, prophet of Arabia in the sixth century A.D.

Judaism is the oldest one-god (monotheistic) religion. Originating in Palestine, which was the early home of the Jews, it went with the Jewish people wherever they traveled. The Christian religion is based on the teachings of Jesus Christ. He was born in Palestine between 8 and 4 B.C.

To us, the right to a trial by jury is one of man's most sacred and natural rights. But it took man a long time to reach the point where this right was recognized.

HOW DID TRIAL BY JURY BEGIN?

When the Normans conquered England in 1066, they started a kind of jury. But the men on a jury were not there to listen as witnesses. They were supposed to decide a case on the basis of their own knowledge of the facts.

It was not until the reign of Henry II in the twelfth century that a big change was made. It was decided that the jury must decide a case solely on the evidence heard in court.

And this, of course, is the whole basis of the trial by jury system we have today. Twelve members of the trial jury listen to the evidence given by witnesses, to the arguments of the lawyers, and to the instructions of the judge. They then retire to a room to decide on their verdict. There seems to be no special reason why the number of jurors is 12, simply that Henry II in 1166 so decided and it has been that way since.

Before jury trials, trials were conducted in different ways. One method was "trial by compurgation." This meant that an accused person brought into court a number of neighbors who were willing to swear that he was innocent.

A second method was "trial by ordeal." The accused was subjected to all kinds of ordeals, like plunging his hands into burning oil, or carrying a piece of red-hot iron. If he survived the ordeal, he was declared innocent.

A third method was "trial by combat." Here a man had to do battle and defeat his enemy. If he won, he was innocent!

The Eskimos are just one more kind of North American Indian. They look Mongolian, but no more so than some other native peoples of North and South America.

WHERE DID ESKIMOS COME FROM?

Like the rest of the Indians, the Eskimos came from Asia. It is believed that the first Eskimos came to North America by way of the Bering Strait and Alaska 2,000 to 3,000 years ago.

Some then moved along the western coast of Alaska and then along the southern coast as far as the place where the city of Anchorage now is. Others moved out upon the Aleutian Islands. But most of them moved east along the northern coasts of Alaska and Canada.

The first known meeting of Eskimos and Europeans was around the

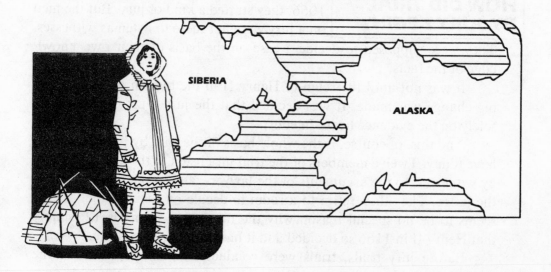

SIBERIA

ALASKA

year A.D. 1000, when the Norse discoverers of America saw Eskimos, probably in Labrador or Newfoundland. The Eskimos later met the Northmen in Greenland.

During the twelfth and thirteenth centuries, there was a great deal of intermarriage between the Europeans and the Eskimos in Greenland. Many of the Eskimos there today are now practically European in appearance.

As a matter of fact, it is important to realize that Eskimos differ among themselves almost as much as Europeans do. Some of them look like blond Scandinavians or Germans. Others look like dark southern Italians.

The reason Eskimos live in the north is probably that they are a hunting people and their country is one of the best for hunting in all of North America.

The Canadian people are made up of different national stocks and races. The first known inhabitants of the country were the Indians.

It is believed the Indians crossed into this continent across the

WHEN DID PEOPLE SETTLE IN CANADA?

Bering Strait and Sea from eastern Asia at least 10,000 years ago. When Europeans first explored the country, Indian bands were living in most of the forested areas. There were only a few Indians in the provinces near the Atlantic Ocean.

The second group of people to enter Canada were the Eskimos. They crossed the Bering Strait from Asia less than 3,000 years ago. There are few records of their early movements.

The first white settlers in Canada were the French. They came in greatest numbers to Quebec, but also to Nova Scotia, where they cleared farms on the southern side of the Bay of Fundy.

The French built their citadel at Quebec City, where the St. Lawrence River narrows, and carved farms out of the forests in the territory. By the time of the British conquest in 1763, there were about 60,000 French in Canada, living chiefly between Quebec and Montreal.

There were not many British in Canada until the American Revolutionary War drove large numbers northward.

Throughout the nineteenth century, thousands of British immigrants came to Canada. The descendants of these peoples from England,

Scotland, and Ireland now make up about half the population.

Around the turn of the century, immigrants came in increasing numbers from Europe, and the largest numbers came from central and eastern Europe—Germans, Czechs, Poles, Rumanians, and Ukranians.

To us it seems so natural to put up an umbrella to keep the water off when it rains. But actually the umbrella was not invented as protection against rain. Its first use was as a shade against the sun!

WHEN WAS THE UMBRELLA INVENTED?

Nobody knows who first invented it, but the umbrella was used in very ancient times. Probably the first to use it were the Chinese, way back in the eleventh century B.C.!

We know that the umbrella was used in ancient Egypt and Babylon as a sunshade. And there was a strange thing connected with its use: it became a symbol of honor and authority. In the Far East in ancient times, the umbrella was allowed to be used only by royalty or by those in high office.

In Europe, the Greeks were the first to use the umbrella as a sunshade. And the umbrella was in common use in ancient Greece. But it is believed that the first persons in Europe to use umbrellas as protection against the rain were the ancient Romans.

During the Middle Ages, the use of the umbrella practically disappeared. Then it appeared again in Italy in the late sixteenth century. And again it was considered a symbol of power and authority. By 1680, the umbrella appeared in France, and later on in England.

By the eighteenth century, the umbrella was used against rain throughout most of Europe. Umbrellas have not changed much in style during all this time, though they have become much lighter in weight. It wasn't until the twentieth century that women's umbrellas began to be made in a whole variety of colors.

Today, of course, it is almost impossible for us to imagine living without electricity. But man has been able to use electricity only since 1800.

In 1800, Alessandro Volta invented the first battery, and so gave

WHEN DID MAN FIRST USE ELECTRICITY?

the world its first continuous, reliable source of electric current. Soon it was discovered that an electric current can be used to produce heat, light, chemical action, and magnetic effects.

Volta's discovery that there is a continuous "flow" of electricity was a great step forward. Various types of machines had been developed, but they would only provide a surge of electricity. Volta's discovery led to many developments in the use of electricity.

Sir Humphry Davy found that electric currents would decompose various substances in solution. From these experiments have come processes that led to the production of low-cost aluminum, pure copper, chlorine, various acids and fertilizers, and special steels.

Then it was discovered that magnetism could be produced by an electric current. A coil of wire through which an electric current is passing acts like a bar magnet. This discovery led to all kinds of electrical devices in which some kind of mechanical motion is produced.

Later on, Michael Faraday found a way to do the opposite—produce electric fields by magnets in motion. This eventually led to the development of electric dynamos and transformers.

So you see that man began to use electricity for practical purposes only recently in his history—and new discoveries and developments are still taking place.

There are several fascinating things about this famous symbol of America's history. One is that it was not called the Liberty Bell until it was about 100 years old. The other is that, in a sense, it has always been cracked!

HOW DID THE LIBERTY BELL BECOME CRACKED?

The bell was ordered to be made in England by the Pennsylvania Assembly to hang in the new State House (now Independence Hall). It was first called the State House Bell. It arrived in Philadelphia in 1752.

The very first time the bell was struck, the bell cracked! It had to be recast twice before it was repaired, and it was finally hung in the State House in 1753.

The bell rang on July 18, 1776, when Philadelphians celebrated the adoption of the Declaration of Independence. This caught the people's imagination and the bell became a symbol of the American Revolution.

The bell rang again in 1783 to announce that the United States had won independence. From then on, the bell rang on all important patri-

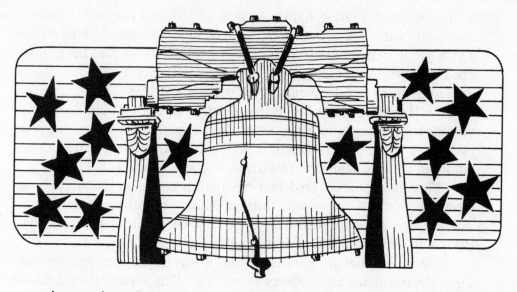

otic occasions. It rang on every July 4th, and to mark the birthdays or the deaths of great men.

In 1835, the bell cracked while tolling the death of Chief Justice John Marshall. After a while, it was repaired. Around this time, the abolitionists (people who wanted to free the Negro slaves) were becoming active in Philadelphia. The sentiment in Pennsylvania was so strong against slavery that the bell was given its present name—the Liberty Bell.

An attempt was made to fix the bell in 1845-1846, but it cracked again as it rang for George Washington's birthday in 1846. This time no one was able to fix it. So it was taken down from the belfry and was finally set upon a framework on the ground floor of Independence Hall tower in 1915.

We assume it is perfectly natural for the government to undertake the job of delivering our letters and packages. But this idea of government service was very slow in developing.

HOW DID THE POSTAL SYSTEM START?

In ancient times in Persia and Rome, the government did arrange for the sending of messages, but these were only concerned with government business. During most of the Middle Ages, merchant guilds and associations and certain universities maintained a limited messenger service for the use of their members.

It was in the sixteenth century that governments began to have regular postal services. They had three chief reasons for doing this. One was to enable them to inspect suspicious correspondence. The second was to produce revenue. And the third was to provide a service for the public. This last reason is practically the only purpose of the postal service today.

Henry VIII had a government postal service in England, and this was enlarged by later rulers. In 1609, no one was allowed to carry letters except messengers authorized by the government. But in 1680, a London merchant started his own penny post for the city and suburbs, and it became quite successful. So the government took it over and continued the service till 1801.

The whole system was finally changed in 1840. Stamps were introduced, and rates made uniform for all distances within the country, varying only according to the weight of the piece of mail. All other countries modeled their postal systems on that of Great Britain.

Just before the days of telegraphs and railways, the United States Government established a mail system that came to be known as the Pony Express. It started in 1860, and ran from St. Joseph, Missouri, to the Pacific coast.

WHAT WAS THE PONY EXPRESS?

To carry the mail, a fleet of horses was used. Each horse would be ridden for 10 to 15 miles, and then the rider would jump on a fresh horse for the next stage. A rider would travel three stages, or 30 miles, before passing on the mail pouch to the next rider.

These riders were tough men with a great deal of courage. They braved all kinds of weather and the danger of attack by Indians to get the mail through. But they actually rode horses, not ponies, so the name "Pony Express" is not accurate!

The dream of a flying machine that would rise straight up is an old one. Leonardo da Vinci made drawings for a gigantic screwlike helicopter about A.D. 1500. He never tried to build one because he had no motor

WHO INVENTED THE HELICOPTER?

to drive it. No one knows where it came from, but a toy helicopter known as "the Chinese top" was shown in France in 1783.

In 1796, Sir George Cayley made experimental forms of Chinese tops and also designed a steam-driven helicopter.

For the next 100 years, a number of people made designs for helicopters. Some were fantastic, others almost practical, and a few of them actually flew. But there were no powerful, lightweight engines. It was not until such engines were made during World War I that anyone made a helicopter that got off the ground with a man aboard.

Igor Sikorsky built two helicopters in 1909 and 1910. One of them actually lifted its own weight. Toward the end of 1917, two Austro-Hungarian officers built a helicopter to take the place of observation balloons. It made a number of flights to high altitudes but was never allowed to fly freely.

Work on helicopters continued in many countries, but none of the machines were what the inventors had hoped for. In 1936, an announcement came from Germany that the Focke-Wulf Company had built a successful helicopter. In 1937 it flew cross-country at speeds close to 70 miles an hour and went up more than 11,000 feet.

In 1940, Sikorsky showed his first practical helicopter and it was delivered to the United States Army in 1942.

A broom and a brush are somewhat alike. A broom, of course, is used for cleaning only, but many brushes serve this purpose too. However, the brush was invented many thousands of years before the broom.

WHO INVENTED THE BROOM?

The cave man used brushes made of a bunch of animal hairs attached to the end of a stick. The kitchen broom was originally a tuft of twigs, rushes, or fibers tied to a long handle. In colonial times in America, this was the kind of broom that was used. And in many parts of Europe today, you can still see streets and floors of homes being swept with such brooms.

The kitchen broom as we now know it is made from stalks of corn, and this kind of broom is an American invention. There is a story about the origin of it that may or may not be true. According to this story, a friend in India sent Benjamin Franklin one of the clothes brushes made and used in that country. It looked very much like a whisk broom.

A few seeds still clung to its straws, and Franklin planted them. They sprouted—and within a few years broom corn was being cultivated.

One day an old bachelor of Hadley, Massachusetts, needed a new broom. He cut a dozen stalks of broom corn, tied them together, and swept out his house. After that he never again used a birch broom.

In fact, he began to make corn brooms and sell them to his neighbors. When he died in 1843, broom making was an important industry, and the town of Hadley was growing nearly a thousand acres of broom corn a year! Today, much of the work of broom making is still done by hand.

Stockings were originally made of leather to cover the legs for protection. But even the idea of protecting the legs in this way was not a common practice until after the beginning of the Christian Era.

WHO INVENTED STOCKINGS?

The first people who tried to make a stocking of any kind like the ones we wear today were the French, and in the seventh century, French men wore leather stockings for protection and warmth.

Soon people began to want to make the stockings more attractive. So fabric stockings appeared, made of pieces of cloth, silk, or velvet sewn together. They were often decorated with gold embroidery, and were worn by fashionable people.

The first knitted worsted stockings appeared in London about the year 1565. Queen Elizabeth received a gift of silk knitted hose which pleased her so greatly that from that time on she wore silk stockings. These silk stockings were made in Italy, and only the very rich could afford them.

It wasn't until the beginning of the twentieth century that silk stockings really became available for the average person to wear.

Thousands and thousands of years ago, primitive man started the custom of using a headpiece of stone to mark the grave of the dead. If we observe what many primitive people do today, and believe it is done for

WHY DO WE HAVE GRAVESTONES?

the same reasons, then the custom seemed to have this purpose: to keep the evil spirits that are supposed to live in dead bodies from rising up!

The gravestone was also a way of warning people away from the spot where those evil spirits lived. Over the centuries, of course, the purpose of a gravestone changed. The Greeks ornamented their gravestones with sculpture. The Hebrews marked their graves with stone pillars. The Egyptians built great tombs and pyramids to mark the places where their dead were buried.

When Christianity appeared, the marking of graves became a common practice. Christianity took over the sign of the cross and ring, which to primitive people was a symbol of the sun. Later on, this was changed to a simple cross, and it is still used today.

There are many types of beards, of course, and each one has a different name for a special reason. A short, pointed beard is called a "Vandyke." This is because the Flemish painter Anthony Van Dyck used to paint

HOW WERE BEARDS NAMED?

men with this kind of beard. The English way of spelling his name was "Van Dyke," and this name soon came to be applied to the kind of beard he had painted!

A "goatee" is just a little bit of a beard on the chin, and the name comes from the fact that it resembles the beard of a he-goat. A tuft of beard under the lower lip is called an "imperial," because Emperor Napoleon III of France used to wear one.

When a man has hair along the cheeks past both ears, he is said to have "burnsides." This is named after a general of the Civil War, General Ambrose Burnside. Sometimes a type of this beard has the name twisted around and is called sideburns!

VANDYKE   BURNSIDE   IMPERIAL

If you had to name the most long-lasting material made by man, would you say it was brick? Well, it happens to be so, and brick will outlast granite, limestone, or even iron!

WHEN WAS BRICK FIRST USED?

Brick, of course, is a modern building material. It is being used today everywhere in the world. But actually, brick is as old as the history of civilization! The Babylonians and Egyptians made and used bricks at least 3,000 years before the birth of Christ. Some excavations suggest that it was used even earlier.

The making of brick in early times was very crude. Brick is made of clay or shale and baked or burned at a high temperature. In early times, raw clay was used to make brick, but no machinery to make it had been invented. The clay was crushed and mixed with water by workmen who trampled it with their bare feet. Straw was mixed with the wet clay to hold the bricks together. The mixture was then formed by hand into different sizes and shapes and placed in the sun to dry.

This crude method was followed for many years until it was discovered that burning the clay with fire made the bricks much harder and better able to withstand dampness. Straw was then no longer needed.

Bricks were first brought to the United States from England as ballast for boats. Soon after the settlement of Virginia and Massachusetts, small kilns were set up. Machines to make brick were invented about 1880 in England.

Almost everybody loves some sort of melon, whether it be muskmelon, honeydew melon, or watermelon. And when something is so popular today, it is hard to believe that it has actually been known and enjoyed for thousands and thousands of years!

WHERE DID MELON ORIGINATE?

The melon is a native of Asia, which means that it grows there without being planted by man. It is quite probable that many thousands of years ago the melon was introduced into other countries. The ancient Egyptians had the melon as one of their delicacies. The ancient Romans and probably the Greeks too enjoyed melons as much as we do! The first people to cultivate the melon in modern times were the French, and that was more than 300 years ago.

Today, melons are an important crop in the United States. Most melons are raised for the local markets, but in the states of California, Colorado, Texas, Georgia, and Florida they are grown by the carloads to be shipped to distant points.

All melons belong to the gourd family. Originally, muskmelons grew in southern Asia and watermelons in tropical Africa. But during centuries of cultivation, they have spread to many countries, and many varieties have been developed from these two types.

Muskmelons get their names from the faint, musky perfume that they have. Muskmelons are also called "cantaloupes." Casaba melons are large, with smooth, yellowish-green rinds. They ripen late in the season and pack and keep better than other melons.

Honeydew melons have a very smooth rind and their flesh is a deep green. Watermelons are much larger than muskmelons, and much juicier.

Man has been skating in one way or another for more than 500 years! Ice skating is much older than roller skating, since roller skating goes back only to the eighteenth century.

WHO INVENTED SKATING? Wheeled skates were used on the roads of Holland about 200 years ago, and we cannot really know who was the first to make them or use them. A man in New York called J. L. Plimpton invented the four-wheeled skate in 1863. It worked on rubber pads and these were the skates that really made this sport popular.

The next development was roller skates with ball bearings. The wheels of roller skates were first made of turned boxwood, but the edges of the wooden wheels broke too easily. Soon wheels were made of hard composition or of steel. Roller skate races were popular in most United States cities until about 1910, when motorcycle and automobile races took their place. But, of course, roller skating has remained a favorite sport with young people.

Ice skating goes back beyond the sixteenth century. At that time the Norsemen bound runners made of bone to their feet and skimmed over the icy surfaces.

Iron runners were next used in skating, followed by the steel runners of today. In early days, the skate-runner was attached to the foot by leather thongs. Later, the skate was clamped and strapped to the shoe. In the modern skate the blade is permanently attached to the skating shoe.

You may think that skiing is a modern sport, but it is actually one of the oldest forms of travel known to man! The word itself comes from the Icelandic word *scidh,* which means "snowshoe" or "piece of wood."

HOW DID SKIING BEGIN?

Some historians claim that skiing goes back to the Stone Age, and they have found ancient carvings that show people on skis. Long before Christianity appeared, the ancient Lapps were known in Scandinavia as *Skrid-Finnen,* or "sliders." They even had a goddess of ski, and their winter god was shown on a pair of skis with curved toes!

The first skis of which there is any record were long, curved frames, often made of the bones of animals, and held to the foot by thongs. And there is a picture carved on stone that is 900 years old that shows a ski runner.

Skiing as a sport began in Norway, in the province of Telemark. In fact, the town of Morgedal in this Norwegian province is known as "the cradle of skiing." Because this region would be snowbound for long periods at a time, it was necessary to use skis to get about. In winter, when the natives went hunting or trapping in the mountains, or to neighboring villages to market or to visit, they had to depend on skis.

And if you think skiing meets are a modern development, it may surprise you to know that in Norway they were having skiing competitions for prizes way back in 1767!

Wrestling is one of the earliest sports known to man. Many hundreds of scenes of wrestling matches are sculptured on the walls of ancient Egyptian tombs. And they show practically all the holds and falls known to us

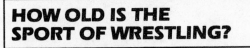

HOW OLD IS THE SPORT OF WRESTLING?

today. So wrestling was a highly developed sport at least 5,000 years ago!

Wrestling as an organized and scientific sport was probably introduced into Greece from Egypt or Asia. But there is a Greek legend that it was invented by the hero Theseus.

Wrestling was an important branch of athletics in ancient Greece. The Greek wrestlers used to rub oil on themselves and then rub fine sand on the oil, to afford a better hold. The champion wrestler of the ancient world was Milo of Croton, who scored 32 victories in the national games, and had six Olympic victories.

In Japan, where wrestling is very popular, the first recorded wrestling match took place in 23 B.C. The Japanese have a style of wrestling called "Sumo," in which weight is very important. Some Sumo champions have weighed as much as 300 pounds, and were tremendously strong—but still quite light on their feet.

In Britain, wrestling was cultivated even in earliest times. Did you know that King Henry VIII liked wrestling and was considered to be very good!

Some form of handkerchief has been used by man since the very earliest times. Probably the first form of handkerchief was the tail of a jackal which was mounted on a stick. Primitive people used this both as a handkerchief and a fan.

HOW LONG HAVE HANDKERCHIEFS BEEN USED?

We know that many savage races made little mats of straw which they wore on their heads and used to wipe away perspiration. This was probably the chief early use of the handkerchief.

In Greek and Roman times, there were not only handkerchiefs but napkins too. Napkins were used for drying the hands at the table. Handkerchiefs were made out of small linen squares which were put inside the clothes and taken along on trips.

In the seventeenth century in France, handkerchiefs became very elegant. They were made of lace and often decorated with gems. When snuff became popular in the eighteenth century, women began to use handkerchiefs of colored cloth.

Marie Antoinette persuaded Louis XVI of France to issue a law that handkerchiefs had to be square in shape, instead of round, or oval, or oblong!

CHAPTER 5
HOW THINGS ARE MADE

The planets in our solar system, as you know, move in orbits around the sun. A planetarium is a device for showing this motion of the planets in their orbits.

| WHAT IS A |
| PLANETARIUM? |

In the sky, the planets look like stars, but they slowly change their positions among the stars from night to night. Mechanical devices to show these motions have been made for several centuries. The first machines had a number of small balls to represent the planets and the sun. Complicated gears controlled the motions of the balls representing the planets so that they moved around the ball representing the sun just as the real planets move around the real sun.

About 1920, a new kind of planetarium, the Zeiss, was invented in Germany. There are now planetariums of this type in many major cities.

The visitor to a modern planetarium sits in a circular theatre with several hundred chairs and sees overhead a wonderfully accurate and beautiful artificial sky. At the center of this room stands the planetarium instrument, which is a complicated machine made up of more than 100 "stereopticons," a special type of projector. These projectors are like those used in motion picture theatres, except that there is no motion in the separate pictures which each projector throws on the dome-shaped ceiling above the audience.

Some of the pictures show the stars, and these pictures are very carefully fitted together on the dome so that they form a single picture, a nearly perfect one of the night sky. Other projectors, like small searchlights, throw spots of light on the dome for the sun, moon, and planets.

There are electric motors and very complicated gears to move these projectors to show the motions of the sun, moon, and planets among the stars. The heavens can be shown as seen from any place on the earth at any time in the past, present, or future.

A telescope is used in looking at distant objects on earth and in studying the stars and other heavenly bodies.

A telescope works by gathering light sent from an object—more light

HOW DO TELESCOPES MAKE THINGS APPEAR CLOSER?

than the naked eye can gather—and focusing it to a tiny, sharp point. This point is then magnified to an image which seems very large and close to the observer.

There are two main types of telescopes, the "refracting" and "reflecting." The refractor uses a lens and the reflector uses a mirror to gather light. In a refractor, the observer looks directly at the object. In a reflector he looks at its reflection in a mirror. In both kinds of telescopes, objects are seen upside down. Another lens may be added to the eyepiece to turn the image right side up, but this is not necessary for studying stars.

The refracting telescope has a closed tube. In the top of the tube is the "object glass," made of two or more lenses, through which passes the light from the object. This light is "refracted" (bent) by the lenses to a bright, sharp focus at the lower end of the tube, where the eyepiece is located. The eyepiece then acts like an ordinary magnifying glass and enlarges this bright image.

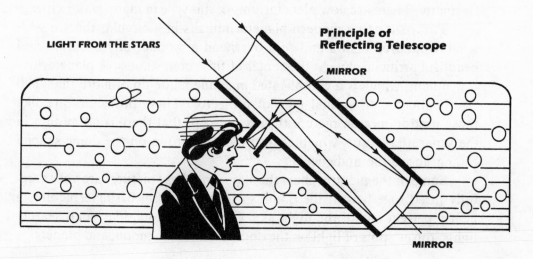

LIGHT FROM THE STARS

Principle of Reflecting Telescope

MIRROR

MIRROR

The reflecting telescope needs only one lens in the eyepiece. Its tube is usually a skeleton framework, open at the top. At the lower end of the tube is a mirror made of glass coated with silver or aluminum and shaped like a large, shallow dish.

Light from a star or other distant object is gathered by this mirror and "reflected" to a bright, sharp focus. A smaller mirror at this focal point sends the image to an eyepiece or camera located at the side of the tube.

What keeps a satellite going in orbit? To understand this we must go back to a certain principle formulated by Sir Isaac Newton back in the seventeenth century. It is known as Newton's First Law of Motion and it says

HOW DO SATELLITES STAY IN ORBIT?

that "every body persists in a state of rest, or of uniform motion in a straight line, unless compelled by external force to change its state."

Now let's see how this applies to a rocket shot into the air. According to Newton's law, it should continue in "uniform motion in a straight line" unless forced to change by some external force. What is that external force? It is the force of the earth's gravity, which pulls all things toward the center of the earth. So instead of flying off into space in a straight line, the rocket is pulled down toward the center of the earth.

Gravity pulls it down at the rate of 14 feet per second. The earth, however, is curved. So as the rocket falls, the earth curves away from it. Now if the rocket is traveling at a speed of 17,000 miles an hour (or 4.7 miles a second), its falling toward the earth will be balanced by the curving away of the earth's surface. In this way, even though it keeps falling, it will keep going around the earth in orbit.

But now something else comes into play—friction. Since the rocket has not gone high enough to escape from the atmosphere around the earth, the force of friction will be slowing it up and thus changing that "balance." As a result, the rocket-satellite will finally fall back to earth.

If a rocket does escape from the earth's atmosphere and from the pull of the earth's gravity, then it comes under the pull of the sun's gravity, and it then goes into orbit around the sun. But since there is no atmosphere there, and therefore no friction to slow it up, it can continue in orbit around the sun forever!

A spectroscope is simply a machine used to take pictures of a spectrum. These pictures are called spectrographs. By using a spectroscope, an astronomer can tell you what a star is made of that is billions of miles

away. He can not only tell you the elements present in that star, but what its temperature is, how fast it is moving, and whether it is moving toward or away from the earth!

All of this is possible because of the fact that white light is really made up of many different colors. When you shine white light through a prism (a triangular piece of glass), it is split up into a band of colors like a rainbow. This is known as the spectrum.

In 1814, a man called Joseph von Fraunhofer looked at the spectrum through—of all things—a telescope! He noticed that all across the spectrum there were hundreds of parallel lines, and he carefully mapped the exact positions of many of these dark lines as they appeared on the spectrum. These are still known as "Fraunhofer lines."

What is the meaning of these lines? Each chemical element in a gaseous or vaporous state has its own pattern of lines occupying its own place in the spectrum. The lines stand for the colors taken up from the sunlight by the element when it is heated to the point that it glows.

This gave scientists a way to find out the materials present in any substance, no matter how far away. Each element always makes its own "dark line," different from those of any other element. By simply comparing the spectrum of a material being studied with the spectra of elements already known in the laboratory, a scientist can tell what it is.

Man has always recognized this need to measure. Problems arose, however: how can we measure heavier, taller, farther, and so on. Units of measurement were needed that everyone would recognize and that could

be used easily. If you wanted to measure the distance between two cities, for example, you would want a fairly large unit such as a mile.

In ancient times, the units of measure were not very exact. They were developed in most cases from familiar things or the human body, just as you might "step off" a distance or measure by means of your hand. In Rome and elsewhere, people used the length of a man's foot to measure length. But since every man's foot differs in size, at one time in the Roman Empire there were 200 different lengths for the foot!

Other units of measurement were just as inexact. The width of a finger or the length of the index finger to the first joint, was the origin of our inch. The yard was the length of a man's arm. The length of a thousand paces (a pace was a double step) was used for long distances and became our mile.

The measuring stick used to build the pyramids in Egypt was two cubits long. A cubit was the length of the arm from the elbow to the end of the middle finger.

Today, it is necessary to have very exact units of measurement. The Congress of the United States has the right to fix the standards of weights of measures for this country. At Washington, D. C., there is a National Bureau of Standards which keeps the standard units of measure to which all others must be compared.

Most of us never have an occasion to make very small measurements. But in building certain types of machines and in other work a difference of 1/1,000 of an inch can be quite important.

WHAT IS A MICROMETER?

To make these kinds of measurements, machinists use what is called a "micrometer." The name comes from the Greek words meaning "small measure." With the help of a micrometer, instruments can be constructed that will be accurate within 1/1,000,000 of an inch!

In measuring the thickness of an object, the object is placed between a fixed rest and one end of the spindle, or screw. The spindle is forced against the object by being turned. In this way, for example, the thickness of a piece of paper can be measured. There are scales that show how far the spindle is from the fixed rest, giving the thickness of the object.

The most common type of micrometer is operated by a screw which has 40 threads to the inch. So each turn of the screw moves the measuring spindle 1/40 of an inch.

A scale, which revolves with the screw, is divided into 25 parts. It therefore indicates the fractions of a turn in units of 1/1,000 of an inch. Such a micrometer might also have what is called a "vernier" scale. On this scale a movement of 1/10,000 of an inch can be read.

Micrometer readings are usually written as decimals or as "mils." The thickness of an ordinary sheet of newspaper, for example is about .0035 inch or 35 mils.

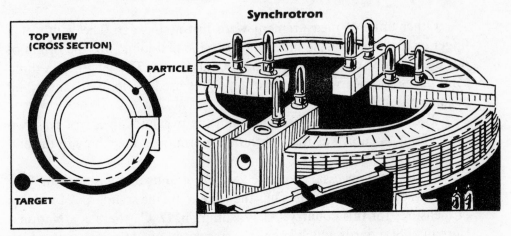

Synchrotron

TOP VIEW
(CROSS SECTION)

PARTICLE

TARGET

**Particle goes round and round until it reaches
peak energy and whirls out toward the target.**

First, what is an atom? Strangely enough, science still does not have the complete answer to this question. What is known about atoms is constantly changing. In fact, atom-smashing machines are providing new information about the atom all the time.

WHAT IS AN ATOM SMASHER?

At one time, an atom was thought to be the tiniest possible particle of matter. Now we know that an atom consists of even smaller particles—there are more than 20 different particles in the core of the atom! Basically, we might say that the atom consists of a heavy, central core (the nucleus) and its related electrons. The basic particles in the nucleus are known as protons and neutrons, and surrounding the nucleus are electrons.

When the structure of an atom is disturbed, some very curious things may happen. Energy may be given off, or the atoms may turn into other elements. When it was discovered that this could happen, the age of atom-smashing began. For example, when protons were speeded up and driven into certain atoms (like bullets being fired into an object) the atoms were broken up, or "smashed."

Soon the search was on for new atomic "bullets." When deutrons (the nucleus of an atom of a substance called deuterium) were fired into atoms, new kinds of changes took place in the elements. A particle of the original atom might be "knocked out," and the atom would become an atom of an entirely different element. Also, great amounts of energy might be released.

Machines were soon developed to shatter atoms. One machine developed is called a "cyclotron." It uses a powerful electromagnet to make high speed protons or deutrons move round and round in a spiral path. Now there are even stronger machines for hurling particles ·into the nucleus of the atom, called "betatrons" and "synchrotrons." These machines enable particles to break into the nucleus of the atom with greater force and accuracy.

Men have developed certain fairly good methods to look for and find oil. But first, how does oil get into the ground to begin with?

Scientists think that petroleum was formed from plants and animals

HOW IS OIL LOCATED UNDERGROUND?

that lived ages ago in and around warm seas that covered much of the earth. As the plants and animals died, they piled up on the sea bottom. In time, millions of tons of sand and mud covered them. Under pressure, the mud and sand changed to rock. The plants and animals turned to a dark liquid trapped in the pores of the rock.

So when men go looking for oil, they know that it is most likely to be found in rocks that used to be the bottoms of old seas. However, oil does not collect in all these rocks. It collects in places called "traps." An oil trap consists of porous rock between layers of nonporous rock. The oil collects in tiny spaces in the rock.

The oil hunter searches for oil traps in several ways, using scientific instruments. These instruments do not actually show whether there is oil, they only help the oil hunter locate what may be an oil trap.

One of the instruments is a gravity meter. Heavy rocks pull harder,

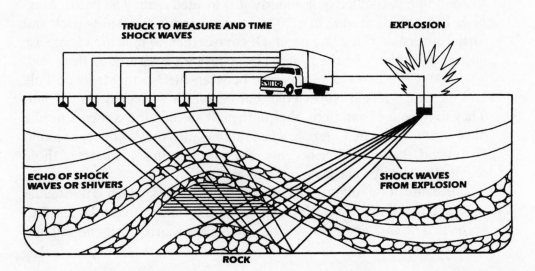

TRUCK TO MEASURE AND TIME SHOCK WAVES

EXPLOSION

ECHO OF SHOCK WAVES OR SHIVERS

SHOCK WAVES FROM EXPLOSION

ROCK

or have a greater force of gravity, than light rocks. The gravity meter gives clues to underground formations by measuring the "pull" of buried rocks.

A magnetometer, which measures variations in the earth's magnetic field, may also be used to gain information on underground rock formations. But the most widely used method for searching for oil is to make a small earthquake by setting off a charge of dynamite. Then the earth's shivers, which travel faster through some types of rock than they do through others, are timed and measured.

But there is still no guarantee after all these measurements that oil will actually be found in any particular spot!

Most people assume a compass needle points "north." And by this they really mean the geographical North Pole. Well, a compass obviously does point in a northerly direction, but not to the North Pole.

WHERE DOES A COMPASS REALLY POINT?

All compass needles in the Northern Hemisphere point to a place known as the North Magnetic Pole. This is located on a peninsula called the Boothia Peninsula, and it is at the northernmost point of the Arctic Coast of North America. It was discovered by Sir James Clark Ross in 1831.

In the Southern Hemisphere, all compass needles point to the South Magnetic Pole, which is located in Antarctica, south of Australia. By the way, a curious thing about the North Magnetic Pole is that it is impossible to point to a particular spot and say it is located here. The North Magnetic Pole travels around in a 20-mile circle, and it even shifts back and forth between morning and night. Of course, that 20-mile area is precise enough a location when considered from distant places around the world.

Today, we know the difference between the North Magnetic Pole and the geographical North Pole, but people in ancient times did not. They lived so far from both, that to them it seemed the compass needle always pointed north. Later on, when sailors sailed the Arctic seas around Greenland, that difference became very puzzling. In some parts of those regions the compass needle points almost west!

Because of this difference between the two poles, which is noticeable in most parts of the world, ship captains sail by charts that take this into account. The captain of the ship may make allowance for it and sail in a true direction.

Sand is really a collection of tiny rocks. Sand is the result of the breakup of the solid rock surfaces of the earth during a period of millions of years. Some rock fragments undergo a chemical action or become dissolved into

WHAT IS SAND?

a fine powdery mass that becomes soil. The fragments that are too hard or could resist the chemical action remain gritty particles that we call sand. Each particle may be from a tenth to a hundredth of an inch in diameter.

In the breakup of ancient rocks, pieces of gravel would be picked up by floods and rivers and they would be rolled along down into the valleys and river beds. As they rolled, many of the gravel pebbles were cracked and gradually they became worn down into grains of sands.

If you look at sand under a magnifying glass, you will notice that there can be quite a collection of different particles. Those that are smooth and well-rounded have either traveled a long distance or have been churned around by the surf on the shore of an ocean. The particles with sharper edges have splintered off more recently and have not traveled very far.

Usually, each grain of sand is composed of only one mineral. But if you pick up a handful of sand, there may be a variety of minerals in it. The most common mineral in sand is quartz.

If there are iron compounds in the sand, it may have interesting colors. Some sands contain rare minerals such as gold, zircon, and garnet. The "white sands" of New Mexico are nearly pure gypsum.

Some sand is so firm and hard-packed that it can be used as a track for auto racing. This firmness is caused by the presence of just enough water to fill the spaces between the grains.

Salt is one of the most common minerals. Chemically, salt (or sodium chloride), is a compound of sodium and chlorine. The common salt we use at home is produced in various ways: from sea water, or the water of

WHAT IS SALT?

salt lakes, from salt springs, and from deposits of rock salt.

A gallon of ordinary sea water contains about a quarter of a pound of salt. Some salt lakes, such as the Dead Sea or Great Salt Lake, contain even larger percentages of salt.

Beds of rock salt are found in various parts of the world and are sometimes hundreds of feet thick. They were probably formed by the evaporation of ancient seas, whose bottoms were later covered by layers of mud and sand. Salt springs may have been formed by the filtering of water through these beds of rock salt.

Most commercial salt is made from rock salt. Wells are drilled down to the salt beds. Pure water is pumped down to the rock salt through a pipe. The water dissolves the salt. The brine, or salt water, is forced up to the surface through another pipe.

After the salt has been brought up in the form of brine, it is evaporated by steam in open pans or in vacuum pans until it forms grains. These grains are dried and then graded. Table salt has a very fine grain. Salt today has many uses in industry, such as in the manufacture of glass, soap, and leather.

Pepper comes from the fruit or seeds of a shrub which originally grew on the western coast of India. Today, however, we get more than 80 per cent of our pepper from the East Indies, mainly Indonesia.

HOW IS PEPPER MADE?

While pepper can grow wild, most of it is cultivated on plantations. The pepper plants require quite a bit of care. They require constant trimming and fertilization, and underbrush must be cut away. The fruit is green at first, then yellow, and turns red when it is ripe. A pepper shrub will yield fruit in three years, and in seven years it will reach full production.

The pepper berries are picked when they turn red, but just before they are quite ripe. This is because they are more pungent in this condition. They are then spread out to dry in the sun. After they are dried, they turn black. Then it is a simple matter of grinding them to obtain ordinary black pepper.

White pepper is not as strong as the black. It is made of ripe berries from which the outer coat has been removed before grinding.

Other types of "pepper," such as Cayenne pepper, paprika, and tabasco pepper, are not related to ordinary black pepper except by taste. The red peppers belong to an entirely different plant. There are many varieties of these and they vary greatly in size. The small red types contain a substance which is very hot or burning to the taste. In the United States, we grow the large "bell" peppers, which are quite mild and are often stuffed to make a variety of tasteful dishes.

Strange as it may seem, nobody really knows what decides the taste of any given thing. We know what taste is produced by certain substances and combinations, but the "law" which determines what the taste of any

WHY IS SUGAR SWEET?

given substance should be is still not understood.

The effect a food has on our taste nerves is connected in some way with its chemical constitution. For instance, when hydrogen ions are present, there is likely to be a sour taste. Amino acids have a sweet taste. Sugar has the kind of acids, or chemical composition, that makes us feel it tastes sweet.

More than 2,000 years ago, Democritus, a Greek philosopher, said that the taste of foods depends on the kind of atoms they throw off. Surprisingly enough, his statement is considered correct today! Unless a substance is in solution, so that the atoms can move about freely, we cannot taste it. We cannot taste a glass marble!

Our taste buds are able to register four sensations: sweet, saline, bitter, and sour. But our tongue is not equally sensitive at all points to all four tastes. The tip of our tongue is sensitive to sweet tastes, the back is more sensitive to bitter, and the sides react to sour and salt tastes.

There is really no such thing as "pure" taste. Our tongue does not just react to sweetness or saltiness, it also is sensitive to weight, roughness or smoothness, temperature, mildness, and other factors. The combination of all these sensations results in what we call the taste of food.

Most of us think of milk simply as a food. And milk is about the most nearly perfect food known to man. But did you know that there are many uses for milk that have nothing to do with food?

WHAT PRODUCTS ARE MADE FROM MILK?

In each quart of milk there is about a quarter of a pound of food solids. One of these solids is casein, or curd.

The casein in skim milk has recently begun to be used in many interesting ways.

The milk is treated with acids to remove the casein. The curd that forms is then dried and powdered. Powdered casein is used in medicines and for beauty preparations. It is used to coat paper and yarn, to waterproof paper and cloth, and to make glue, paint, and putty.

When the powder is moistened and mixed with certain chemicals, it forms a plastic. In this form it is used to make combs, knife and brush handles, buttons, and toys.

Today, milk undergoes many processes before it reaches our table. It is pasteurized (heated to a high temperature) to kill any harmful bacteria that may be in the milk. It is homogenized, which means it is forced through a small opening under high pressure. This breaks up the fat globules into very small particles and scatters them through the milk so the fat will not rise to the surface.

In many areas, milk is fortified with Vitamin D. And then, of course, there are many new ways of preserving milk, since milk cannot be kept fresh for long periods. One way is to remove the water from the milk and make it into powdered milk. Another way is to remove about half the water by evaporation and make evaporated milk. Still another way is to evaporate milk and add sugar to make sweetened condensed milk.

All cheeses are made basically the same way. A "starter" composed of certain bacteria is added to fresh milk. These bacteria cause the milk to develop a slight acidity, and this is known as "ripening."

HOW MANY KINDS OF CHEESE ARE MADE?

When the ripening has progressed to the proper stage, rennet is added. Rennet is part of the natural digestive juices from a sheep. This causes the formation of a curd, or solid portion. Then the whey (liquid portion) is drawn off, and the curd is salted and

cured. This is a very brief description of the making of cheddar cheese, which is typical.

Cheese is made in all parts of the world today and from many different kinds of milk. More than 400 varieties of cheese are manufactured in Europe, and about 300 in the United States.

Many countries have developed special kinds of cheese which have become popular all over the world. Some of the most famous world cheeses are Cheshire, Cheddar, and Stilton of England; Edam and Gouda of Holland; Roquefort, Camembert, and Brie of France; Parmesan, Gorgonzola, and Bel Paese of Italy; Gruyère and Swiss of Switzerland; Limburger of Belgium.

Today, many people believe that Canada and the United States make cheeses as fine as Europe's. A large part of the Canadian cheese is shipped to England. The United States produces more than 1,000,000,000 pounds of cheese annually, and almost half of it comes from Wisconsin. Other leading cheese-producing states are Illinois, Missouri, New York, Minnesota, and Indiana.

Chemistry is the science used to find out what things are made of and how they can be changed. By change, the chemist means a chemical change.

A chemist works carefully and makes many tests to be certain that

WHAT DOES A CHEMIST DO?

his experiments and discoveries are right. A chemist works on things that are part of the life of everyone in today's world. Chemistry is used in making paper, ink, preservatives for food, and poisons for insects. Chemistry studies the combinations of metals to make alloys. It teaches how to enrich soils and how to make paints.

Chemistry has developed to such an extent, that a chemist today usually specializes in one field of chemistry. Here are the various sections of chemistry in which a chemist can work.

"Organic chemistry" includes all substances that make up the bodies of plants and animals. "Inorganic chemistry" deals with all other compounds found in nature. "Qualitative analysis" shows what an unknown substance is, and what elements and compounds make it up. "Quantitative analysis" breaks up a substance into its simplest parts. It shows how much of each part the substance contains.

"Physical chemistry" deals with problems of both chemical and physical changes. From it is learned such things as why salt makes water more difficult to boil or freeze. "Physiological chemistry" (biochemistry) deals with the chemical changes that go on in living things. "Applied chemistry" finds out how discoveries made in other branches of chemistry can be used.

Being a chemist today means being something of a specialist, because the whole field of chemistry has become so big. One of the most exciting developments in chemistry is that today a chemist can become a creator of new materials. He can take molecules apart and put them together in different ways so that a new compound is produced in his laboratory.

Many people have strange ideas about hypnotism. They believe, for instance, that a hypnotized person might not be able to be awakened. This is not true. They think that a hypnotized person can be made to commit

IS HYPNOTISM DANGEROUS?

crimes or act in ways that are harmful. This is not true either.

There is a kind of danger involved with hypnotism—and that is to have it conducted by an untrained person, one who is not trained in psychology. This is because hypnotism can, in some cases, damage the personality of the subject.

But hypnotism is being used today in medical treatment of the body, in dentistry to prevent people from feeling pain, in surgery, and in psychological treatment of persons.

When a person is hypnotized, he is in a sort of trance that resembles sleep. But there are many degrees of depth in hypnosis. A hypnotized person may be wide awake and know everything that is going on about him. Or he may be in such a deep trance that he knows nothing of what is taking place about him, except the ideas, commands, or suggestions given him by the hypnotist.

These commands and suggestions which the subject will follow can range from standing, walking, shivering, or perspiring. The hypnotist can also make the subject's heart beat faster or slower, and make his face turn white or blush a bright red.

The fascinating thing is that the hypnotist can also control the feelings of the subject. So he can make him hate his favorite food, or like a food he always hated. This change may only last as long as the person is hypnotized, or it may last for several months. In some cases, the change is permanent.

Archimedes was a mathematician and inventor who lived in the ancient Greek colony of Syracuse, Sicily. The king of Syracuse, Hiero, asked Archimedes if he could tell whether the royal golden crown con-

WHAT IS ARCHIMEDES' PRINCIPLE?

tained any silver. Archimedes was puzzled by this problem for a long time. One day as he stepped into his bath he noticed the rise of water. He rushed through the streets crying "Eureka!"

He now knew how to solve Hiero's problem. He first weighed the crown. He then found a lump of gold and a lump of silver, each weighing the same as the crown. Then he dropped the crown into a vessel of water and measured the rise of the liquid. He did the same with the lump of gold. If the crown had been pure gold, the rise would have been the same. But there was a difference, and by also measuring the rise in the water when the lump of silver was dropped into it, Archimedes found the exact proportions of the two metals in the crown.

The law of specific gravity, or Archimedes' Principle, states that any object immersed in a liquid is buoyed up by a force equal to the weight of the liquid displaced.

Archimedes was also the inventor of many scientific devices for use in ancient warfare. When the Romans attacked the city of Syracuse by land and sea in 214 B.C., they were held off for nearly three years by the inventions of Archimedes. He created catapults that were able to hurl huge stones at the Romans. He also wrote books on geometry and physics and knew much about the power of levers.

Archimedes was killed by a Roman soldier during the capture of Syracuse, supposedly while he was absorbed in drawing a mathematical figure.

A boat is a pretty big object, yet it floats easily on the surface of a lake or ocean. Why? Well, something floats in a liquid, or fluid, because the fluid holds it up. The fluid actually offsets the force of gravity, which

WHAT MAKES A BOAT FLOAT?

pulls everything to the center of the earth.

That upward push on a floating object is called "buoyant force," or simply "buoyancy."

This force acts on every object that is in a fluid. If you want to feel this force, just take a blown-up beach ball into the water. The water seems to push up on the ball.

The buoyant force of a liquid acts on objects that cannot float too. For example, a stone feels lighter in your hand underwater than when you hold it in the air.

The buoyant force of a fluid is not always strong enough to lift a solid body. And it is not the weight of the body that decides this. For example, a small stone sinks, but a 100-pound piece of balsa wood floats. Whether a body will sink or float depends on its density. If you compare two blocks of the same size, one made of steel and one made of cork, the block of steel will weigh more, even though it occupies the same amount of space. So the density of steel is greater than that of cork.

Density depends on weight and on size. If two bodies have the same weight, the smaller one is the denser body. Fluids also have density.

When a solid body is placed in a liquid, it pushes some of the fluid aside. If the solid is more dense than the fluid, it weighs more than the fluid it pushes aside, and it will sink. If the solid is less dense than the fluid, it will float.

A ship is a metal shell and contains large quantities of air. The ship as a whole, with air inside, is less dense than water. It weighs less than the water it pushes aside. That is why it floats.

Why can a needle or a thin razor blade be made to float on water? Why can some insects walk on water? Why do soap bubbles act as if they were surrounded by a rubber film?

WHAT IS SURFACE TENSION?

The explanation for all of these is the existence of surface tension. It is called that because the surface of every liquid seems to be under tension, like the tension of a stretched sheet of rubber. The surface tends to shrink to the least possible area.

Surface tension is believed to be caused by the attraction of molecules for one another. Molecules in the surface of a liquid are attracted inward, toward the liquid, more strongly than outward. This is because there are more molecules just beneath the surface than above it.

Molecules in the midst of the liquid are attracted equally in all directions. So the effect does not take place in the midst of a liquid.

If you watch a slowly dripping water faucet, you will see the water gradually extend downward. Surface tension is holding it together. Finally, the weight of the water is too great for the surface tension to support, and a drop separates and falls. The falling drop draws itself into a tiny sphere by surface tension, because a sphere has the smallest possible area for the enclosed volume of water.

Another example of surface tension can be seen when you fill a teaspoon with water right to the very top. Surface tension keeps it from overflowing.

If you rub a glass rod with silk, you will find that small pieces of dry paper jump to the rod and cling to it. The same things happens if you rub a piece of plastic with fur.

WHAT IS STATIC ELECTRICITY?

What has happened to the glass and plastic? Scientists say they acquired an electric charge, that is, they became charged with electricity. And the charges produced by rubbing one material with another are called "static electricity."

"Static" means "at rest," so static electricity is made up of electric charges that are ordinarily at rest. Electricity that travels along wires is electricity in motion. It is called "current electricity."

All matter is made up of tiny particles called "atoms." And each atom is made of even smaller particles. Some of these smaller particles are charged with electricity. There are two kinds of charges: positive (or plus) and negative (or minus). The particles with a positive charge are called "protons." Those with a negative charge are called "electrons."

Normally, a piece of glass has equal numbers of protons and electrons. The positive charges of the protons and the negative charges of the electrons cancel each other out. So there is no net charge on the glass.

But when the glass is rubbed with silk, some of its electrons are pulled away. The glass then has more protons than electrons. It has a net positive charge. This positive charge is equal to the combined charges of the extra protons.

Rubbing plastic with fur gives the plastic a negative charge. This is because electrons are pulled off the fur by the plastic. The plastic has more electrons than protons.

A Greek named Thales, who lived about 600 B.C., was the first to observe static electricity. He rubbed amber with a woolen cloth and found it attracted light objects. But he could not explain why this happened.

Certain fabrics have to be dry cleaned instead of washed with water, because water may shrink or discolor them. Wools, silks, satins, and velvets are examples of such fabrics.

HOW ARE CLOTHES DRY CLEANED?

In dry cleaning, a "solvent" replaces the water. Today, the solvents that are used are synthetics. They dissolve greases, oils, and other dirt in the fabric and then they evaporate.

In a dry-cleaning plant, the garments are placed in a cleaning machine that is very much like a washing machine. But instead of water, a solvent is used. As the machine revolves, the solvent goes through the clothes. Then it goes into a filter to be purified, and back into the machine again. Because solvents are expensive, they are used over and over again.

The solvent is mixed with a detergent that helps to loosen the dirt and float it away. The clothes tumble gently in the mixture until the dirt is washed out. Then they are rinsed in fresh solvent. Detergent is not used in the rinsing.

The machine then spins the clothes at high speed until most of the solvent is removed. A dryer tumbles the clothes loosely in warm air. The warm air helps evaporate the solvent.

After drying, the garments go to a "spotter." His job is to take out stains that are left. To do this he must first find out what the stain is and what chemicals will loosen it. He also tests the fabric to make sure the color will not run. The next step is pressing, and this is usually done by machines, though dresses may be "touched up" with a hand iron.

The first dry-cleaning plant in the world was opened in Paris in 1845. But long before that people were using solvents instead of water to clean certain fabrics. The first solvent to be used was probably turpentine, which is mentioned as a cleaner in a book written in 1690!

Many customs have arisen in the world concerning the bodies of the dead. Among some peoples it was and still is considered very important not to allow the body of the dead person to decay. The art of preserving dead bodies from decay is

WHAT IS EMBALMING?

called "embalming."

It originated in ancient Egypt. The Egyptians preserved certain of their dead as mummies, and from there the custom spread to other parts of the world. From the time of the Middle Ages until about 1700, embalming was carried on in Europe by methods that were somewhat like the ancient Egyptian's. The organs were removed and herbs put in their place, the body was soaked in spirits of wine, cloths soaked in spirits were applied to the body, and there was a final wrapping in waxed or tarred sheets.

During the nineteenth century, embalmers in Europe developed various chemicals which they injected into the body to preserve it. Some of these embalming fluids were: aluminum salts and arsenic; a saturated solution of arsenic; zinc chlorida solution; and bichloride of mercury solution.

Modern embalming actually had its start in the Civil War. Certain experts in the process traveled about the country teaching and demonstrating how to preserve the bodies of the Civil War dead, and so the knowledge spread throughout the United States.

The basic thing that is done is that the embalming fluid replaces the blood of the body, and this helps preserve it. There are laws in all states that prohibit the use of certain chemicals for this purpose, and specify that certain others must be used.

A dam is a wall-like barrier built across a stream valley to block the flow of water. Man has been putting up dams for thousands of years because he finds them useful or necessary. What are some of these uses and needs?

WHY ARE DAMS BUILT?

Some dams direct the water they have blocked into canals, pipelines, or tunnels. These dams supply irrigation, water power, or water supply systems. Dams that raise the level of the water are used to produce water power, or to provide pools deep enough to float boats over obstructions in the stream bed. They may also form ponds or lakes for recreation, such as swimming, fishing, or boating. In some cases, they stop the rise and fall of water due to tides.

Dams are also used to store water for use during the growing season. They are used to meet year-round needs for city water supplies, or to add to low flows in the dry season to make water power more dependable.

Dams are used to improve water conditions in areas that have a great deal of water pollution, or to make streams more attractive for recreation. Dams that are used to store flood waters lessen damages from flooding downstream. But these dams must be emptied as fast as possible after the flood, in order to be ready for another flood.

So you see there are many purposes for building dams. Sometimes a dam is built for a combination of reasons. Many of the dams built in ancient times were simply to supply water for irrigation needs. Many of them were dikes of stone and brush across the stream which directed water into a ditch where it flowed to fields or orchards. Later on, dams were built to provide a fall of water to drive water wheels to grind grain or to operate all kinds of mills.

When light strikes a surface, it is either absorbed (taken in), or reflected (bounces back). A mirror is a smooth surface that reflects light.

What happens is quite simple: light is reflected from a mirror in

HOW DO WE SEE OURSELVES IN A MIRROR?

about the same way that a rubber ball bounces from a wall. If you throw the ball straight forward at the wall, it will come straight back. If you throw it at an angle, it will bounce off at the same angle in the other direction.

When light strikes a mirror at an angle, it bounces back at an equal angle in another direction. The first angle is called "the angle of incid-

ence"; the second is called "the angle of reflection." The two angles are always equal.

The mirror you usually use is called a "plane" mirror, which means it has a flat surface. Curved mirrors do not produce true images, but distort them. A mirror consists of a piece of glass with a coating on the back made of silver nitrate. The silver backing keeps the light from passing through the glass. It is the actual reflecting surface, while the glass is just to protect the soft silver from scratches and tarnish.

Now imagine you are standing before a mirror. Light rays strike your body and are reflected from it. (This is the way we see things. You are able to see objects because light rays are reflected from them.) These light rays strike the mirror and bounce back to your eyes. So you see a clear image of yourself!

But in a mirror you look as though you are really behind the mirror. The image you see is called a "virtual" image, because the light rays seem to come to a focus behind the mirror. You also see yourself reversed. Your right hand appears to be left, and everything else is reversed from one side to the other.

Did you ever wonder why a polar bear is white? Or certain caterpillars are green? Or why a field mouse has a brownish color? Nature is protecting these animals from being detected by their enemies by providing them with "camouflage."

WHAT IS CAMOUFLAGE?

Men noticed long ago that many

animals, birds, and insects were concealed from their enemies or sometimes their prey by a coloring which resembled their surroundings. But no one thought of applying this principle to the benefit of man. With the coming of modern warfare, and the need to conceal a great many troops and targets, camouflage began to be applied to man.

Actually, a beginning in this direction was made in India about the middle of the nineteenth century. Instead of having soldiers wear the brilliant red and blue uniforms then in use, they were dressed in earth-colored uniforms and were thus harder to detect.

This idea was developed in many ways. Soldiers in most armies were given uniforms whose colors helped them remain concealed. When warships were painted gray all over, the idea was the same. It made the ship harder to see in the water.

The word "camouflage" comes from a French word meaning "to disguise." The art of camouflage did not make much progress until the days of World War I. During this war, camouflage became an important part of providing protection and it was applied to almost every branch of military and naval service.

During World War II, camouflage became more important than ever and was used to protect factories and bridges as well as men.

A share of stock in a company is a share in the ownership of the company. The company issues "stock certificates" in order to raise money for its needs and for growth. Stockholders share in the company's profits by receiving payments called "dividends."

HOW DOES THE STOCK MARKET WORK?

When a company continues to grow and issues more stock, it might ask to be "listed" on the New York Stock Exchange. This means that it will have the right to have its stock bought and sold, or "traded" at the Exchange. So the stock exchange is a market place for stocks and bonds.

The prices of stocks and bonds are not regulated by anyone. They are determined only by their value to the people who want to buy and sell. The prices depend on how much buyers are willing to pay for a stock, and how cheaply owners are willing to sell.

The actual buying and selling is done by a "broker," who acts as an agent or representative for the people who want to buy and sell stocks. The broker carries out his customers' orders for which he gets a small percentage of the sale or purchase price, which is known as a "commission." Commission rates are set by the Exchange, so all brokers charge the same rates.

Most stockholders give their orders to buy and sell to their brokers over the telephone. But some go directly to the "brokerage office." Here, on the "ticker tape," they can see every purchase and sale of every stock listed on the New York Stock Exchange in units of 100 shares.

The development of the match has a very long history. Even the cave man had a way of starting a fire. He would strike a spark from a flint.

The Egyptian twirled his bow drill on a piece of wood and by this

WHAT MAKES A MATCH LIGHT?

friction lighted his fire. The Greek rubbed pieces of bay and buckthorn together. The Roman struck two flinty stones together and caught the spark on a sulfured splint of wood. During the Middle Ages, sparks struck by flint and steel were caught on charred rags, dried moss, or fungus.

Modern matches were made possible by the discovery of phosphorus, an element that burns at a low temperature. Today, of course, we have two types of matches in common use. One is the friction match, which can be lighted on any rough surface. The second is the safety match, which can be lighted by rubbing it on a specially prepared surface.

The friction match is made by first dipping the match into a solution of ammonium phosphate. The chief reason for this is to prevent "afterglow." Then the match head is dipped into melted paraffin, and next into a paste containing glue, lead oxide, and a compound of phosphorus.

The match lights because friction causes the phosphorus and lead compounds to explode. This sets fire to the paraffin, and this then sets fire to the wood.

In the safety match, the tip contains two chemicals, antimony sulfide and potassium chlorate. The side of the box you rub it on contains red phosphorus. The material on the tip of the match will not ignite easily unless it is rubbed on this prepared surface. The friction produced by the rubbing vaporizes a little of the red phosphorus, which ignites and sets fire to the tip of the match.

Licorice is a product made from the long, sweet root of a plant that belongs to the pea family. The scientific name of this plant is *Glycyrrhiza glabra*. The word *glycyrrhiza* means "sweet root," and if you keep saying

WHAT IS LICORICE?

that word long enough you'll see how we came to get the word "licorice"!

The plant grows three to five feet tall, with pale blue, pealike flowers, and leaves of 9 to 17 leaflets. The licorice plant is a native of southern Europe and western Asia. Today, it is cultivated chiefly in Italy, Spain, and the Soviet Union.

The United States imports large quantities of licorice, although some is grown in Louisiana and California. The plants are raised from seed or from root divisions. Along the Mediterranean coast of Europe, the growing and production of licorice is quite an important industry.

Roots are dug when the plants are three years old. When they are harvested, they are full of water, so they must be dried out for six months to a year. The dried roots are then cut into pieces six inches to a foot long, sorted, and baled.

To prepare licorice, the roots are crushed and boiled. The liquid that remains is then evaporated. This leaves a paste or black stick licorice. These licorice sticks are made from the paste mixed with a little starch so they will not melt in warm weather.

Licorice is used in medicines as a cough remedy, as a laxative, and to make some medicines taste better. In France, Egypt, and some other countries, the root extract is used to make a cooling drink!

The economic system in the United States is sometimes called capitalism. It is more accurately described as a system of free enterprise. Under communism, all industry is taken over by the government. In the free enter-

WHAT IS CAPITALISM?

prise system the plant, machinery, and other equipment used by industry is the property of private citizens.

Business may be carried on by a single person, by two or more people in a partnership, or by corporations. Large-scale industries are usually operated by corporations in which many individuals have bought shares of stock or have invested their money.

Businesses are operated by their owners for the sake of profit, or a return, above cost of production, which may or may not be realized.

Capital and credit—the money funds needed to build plants, pay wages, and purchase machinery and raw materials—are supplied by such institutions as banks and insurance companies. Industry has to pay interest for the use of these funds. This interest is part of the cost of production.

Although the main necessities for living under the system of free enterprise are supplied by private business, some important needs are taken care of by government. Schools are maintained by local and state governments. In many cities and states, the streetcar lines and the gas, electricity, and water works are publicly owned. The federal government runs the postal system. Some of these services have to be paid for by taxes levied upon the general public, while others are supplied at a price to users.

Have you ever wished you could pick up a stone from the ground and change it into a diamond? Or hold a piece of metal in your hand and have it suddenly become pure gold?

WHAT IS ALCHEMY?

Men have had just such wishes since the earliest times. And they actually tried to do something about it! Alchemy is the so-called art or science of trying to change base (the less valuable) metals, such as mercury and lead, into gold and silver. It was practiced for many centuries.

An old myth says that alchemy was first taught to man by the fallen angels. The Greeks and Arabs were the first alchemists. From them the

interest in this imaginary art spread to western Europe, where it reached its peak in the Middle Ages. Since changing other metals to gold and silver held out the promise of limitless wealth, many people gave everything they had to the alchemists in the hope they would make them rich. And the false promises of the alchemists took many a fortune from such victims.

In castles and dungeons, strange men shouted weird words over boiling pots in the hope of finding the great secret. Some alchemists tried to produce gold from mercury alone, while others mixed mercury with sulphur, arsenic, or sal ammoniac.

Later on, alchemy included the search for a magic substance called "the philosophers' stone," which was believed to have the power of curing all diseases and of making life last forever, as well as of changing base metals into gold.

Although the study of alchemy was not scientific, it gave rise to much valuable information concerning various substances. It may be said that alchemy was the forerunner of chemistry. Many of the alchemists were nothing more than adventurers, but there were a few great men among them who honestly believed in the possibilities of alchemy.

In the first century in China, a method was invented for making paper from the stringy inner bark of the mulberry tree. The Chinese pounded the bark in water to separate the fibers, then poured the soupy mixture

HOW IS PAPER MADE?

onto a tray with a bottom of thin bamboo strips. The water drained away and the soft mat was laid on a smooth surface to dry.

In time, machinery was invented to "beat" the paper-making material to the condition of pulp. Other machinery was devised to squeeze the water out more efficiently. One of the most important events in the history of paper was the invention of a machine to make a continuous sheet, or "web" of paper. This was invented by a Frenchman named Louis Robert in 1798, but two Englishmen, Henry and Sealy Fourdrinier, bought the patent from him and improved the machine. Today the "Fourdrinier" is still the basic machine for making continuous sheets of paper.

Until about 1860, practically all paper was made from rags. Many kinds of paper today are still made from rags, old rope, and burlap. The material is cut into small pieces, boiled and cleaned, and raveled out into threads. A machine then beats them, and other materials are added to give the paper certain qualities. A filler, such as talc, gives the paper a smoother surface.

In making newsprint, book paper, and other papers from wood pulps, a mixture of pulp is prepared which goes to the Fourdrinier to be made into a continuous sheet. Presses squeeze out some of the water, but then it must go to huge, revolving steam-heated drying cylinders which reduce the moisture still more. Then the bare sheet passes through polished rolls which give the paper a smooth, level finish.

Lithography means "stone writing." Actually, it is a simple method of printing. The design to be printed is drawn upon the printing surface. It does not need to be cut or engraved into a plate or raised above the surface of the plate. The subject is

WHAT IS LITHOGRAPHY?

drawn right on a stone.

The best lithographer's stone is a gray, smooth-grained limestone. After the design is drawn on the stone, the stone is dampened with water so that all the surface is wet except the part covered by the greasy ink. Water will not stick to this part. An inking roller, carrying a thick, oily ink, is then rolled over the stone.

Because they are wet, the parts of the stone not covered with the design will not pick up any ink from the roller. The design itself, drawn in greasy crayon, picks up more ink. When the form is ready to print, a

STONE

sheet of paper is pressed against the stone. The sheet picks up the ink from the design, but that is all, for the damp stone around the pattern keeps the ink from spreading or smearing.

Lithography is not a difficult process. All that is needed are a stone, the grease crayons, a sponge to dampen the stone, and a roller to do the inking. If an error is made, the mistake can be wiped from the stone and redrawn.

There is a modern form of lithography that is called "offset printing." Instead of a stone, shiny sheets of zinc and aluminum are used. The subjects to be printed are laid down photographically on these flexible plates. Rotary presses automatically moisten, ink, and print hundreds of impressions per hour.

The Eiffel Tower was designed for the Paris Exposition of 1889. It was intended to be the symbol and main attraction of the exposition, just as most World Fairs have one structure to symbolize it. It is made of beautiful columns of iron latticework, and rises 984 feet in the air.

WHY WAS THE EIFFEL TOWER BUILT?

There are platforms at 190 feet, at 381 feet, and at 906 feet, which can be reached by elevators. A circular staircase continues to a scientific laboratory at the top. In the laboratory, meteorologists study temperatures, air currents, clouds, winds, and rainfall. By international agreement, a wireless station sends time signals into space daily.

You can see the Eiffel Tower from any part of Paris, since most buildings in the city are quite low. As a tourist attraction, the Eiffel Tower is hard to beat. It stands in a beautiful setting and as you go up in the elevator one of the most beautiful cities in the world unfolds before you.

The tower was built by Alexandre Eiffel, who also built many outstanding bridges in various parts of the world. In the city of Nice, France, there is an observatory with a movable dome that he built, and he also built the framework for the Statue of Liberty. Eiffel also invented movable section bridges, and he was the first to study the effects of air currents on planes by using models in an air tunnel.

The Eiffel Tower cost more than $1,000,000 to build. It was paid for by Eiffel except for $292,000 contributed by the government. In payment, Eiffel was allowed to collect visitors' admission fees for 20 years.

In Shakespeare's play *Julius Caesar,* a soothsayer, a person who was supposed to foretell the future, tells Caesar to "beware the ides of March."

This phrase has become so well known that some people imagine it

WHAT IS THE IDES OF MARCH?

means something mysterious. But all it actually means is beware the 15th day of March! The "ides" was the name given in the Roman calendar to the 13th day of the month. There were four exceptions to this: the months of March, May, July, and October. In these months, the ides fell on the 15th day. The soothsayer in the play was predicting that something terrible would happen to Julius Caesar on the 15th day of March—and of course something did. He was assassinated on that day!

The Roman calendar was an interesting combination of confusion and superstition. There were twelve months in this calendar: Martius, Aprilis, Maius, Junius, Quintilis, Sextilis, September, October, November, December, Januarius, and Februarius. March 1st was the official New Year's Day for the Romans until 153 B.C., when the year was declared to start with January 1st.

The Roman calendar was not the same every year, and there was a group of officials who decided how it should work. They were called "the pontifices." Every month they would watch for the new moon. When it was seen, they would proclaim how many days were to be counted before "the nones." This was a special day of the month. The "ides" was the day of the full moon. The first day of the month was called "the calends."

Because each year had a different length, there was great confusion in the calendar. In 46 B.C., Julius Caesar made changes to uniform the calendar. After that, a "Julian" calendar (named after him) was used by most of Europe for hundreds of years.

Man has been replacing missing natural teeth since very ancient times. These artificial teeth were made out of wood, or animal teeth, or even human teeth! Then, at the end of the eighteenth century, a one-piece set

WHAT ARE FALSE TEETH MADE OF?

of porcelain artificial teeth was created for the first time.

At the beginning of the nineteenth century, another great step forward was made. A man called Fonzi, an Italian dentist practicing in Paris, made individual porcelain teeth mounted on gold or platinum bases. Porcelain teeth were introduced into the United States about 1817.

The next step was to improve the appearance of such teeth by making them harmonize with the shape of the face. Before that, false teeth would sometimes change the whole facial expression of the people who wore them and make them look quite peculiar.

Today, people who wear false teeth can look just as they did before. False teeth made out of porcelain, plastics, and glass can be made in such a variety of shapes, sizes, and colors, that they can match perfectly almost any natural teeth. They are usually fastened to plastic bases that look like the natural gums.

About one-fifth of all artificial teeth are made of plastic. They have an advantage over porcelain teeth in that they are less brittle, easier to grind and polish, are more solidly joined to the plastic base, and they make less noise when they are used.

But porcelain teeth wear better and are better for chewing. This is probably the reason that porcelain is still preferred in making false teeth.

Did you know that a thermostat automatically regulates temperature? Now you may not think this is important, but where a thermostat is used it makes a big difference in comfort and efficiency.

HOW DOES A THERMOSTAT WORK?

A thermostat controls the heating of homes and heating devices used in industry. Thermostats also regulate the temperature of such appliances as electric blankets, irons, toasters, clothes dryers, waffle irons, ovens, and water heaters. In an air-conditioning system, thermostats feel warmth and signal for more cold air from the cooling equipment.

How does a thermostat work? Like a thermometer, a thermostat also "feels" temperature changes. A thermometer just shows the changes on a scale, but a thermostat also operates some type of equipment, such as a heating furnace, to maintain temperature at a previously selected point.

For example, if the furnace is to keep your house at a certain temperature, the thermostat dial is set at that point. If the air becomes colder in the house, the thermostat senses, or feels, this and sends an electrical signal to the furnace. This signal causes the furnace to start.

When the room warms to the desired temperature, the thermostat

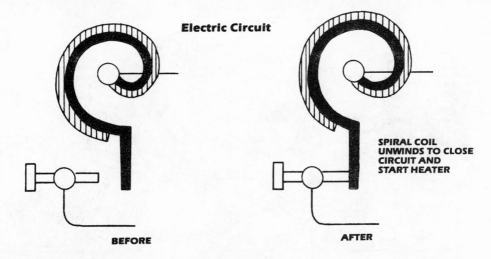

Electric Circuit

BEFORE

AFTER

SPIRAL COIL
UNWINDS TO CLOSE
CIRCUIT AND
START HEATER

automatically sends another signal that stops the furnace. When the room gets cold again, the furnace starts once more.

Instead of using mercury to feel temperature changes (as in a thermometer), thermostats commonly use a strip of specially built metals. These metals always bend at the same rate according to temperature. The bending of the metal strip causes an electrical contact to be broken or made, and the change in the electric current that is made causes a switch to go on or off.

A "fertilizer" is any substance that will increase the growth and yield of plants when added to the soil. If the soil has never been tilled before, it needs little or no fertilizing. But each new crop that grows in a soil draws

WHY ARE FERTILIZERS USED?

valuable chemicals out of it. In time, such soil will be almost worthless for crops unless it is made fertile again.

So the purpose of fertilizer is to return to the soil those valuable chemicals that have been drawn out of it. The most common of all fertilizers, and still the most important one on the average farm, is the manure of animals. It is called the complete fertilizer because it contains three basic elements: nitrogen, phosphorus, and potassium.

Sometimes the soil does not need a complete fertilizer. The soil may be exhausted of only a single element necessary to the growth of crops. Then an incomplete artificial fertilizer is used. It supplies the soil only with those elements in which it is deficient.

Artificial fertilizers are made in a variety of ways, and they work quite well. But they have one drawback. They will greatly enrich the soil during the first few years of their use. After that time, unless certain green crops are plowed under, the artificial fertilizers begin to lose their effectiveness. Plowing under the green crops supplies the soil with organic matter which it needs.

How does a farmer know what elements are lacking in his soil and what fertilizers to use? The individual states and the U. S. Department of Agriculture have laboratories that will test samples of the soil, and their analysis tells the farmer what his soil lacks and the kind of fertilizer that will do the most good.

Fertilizers have been used since very ancient times. The Hindus and Chinese used them, and the North American Indians used to put a dead fish in each hole in which they planted grains of corn.

There are many kinds of sugars in nature, and glucose is the most common of them. It is found in honey and in many fruits, particularly grapes. That is why glucose is often called "grape sugar." Another chemical name for it is "dextrose."

WHAT IS GLUCOSE?

Ordinary sugar, which is cane sugar or beet sugar, is called "sucrose" by chemists. It is a combination of glucose and fructose.

The starch which is so common in plants and which is found in flour, cereals, and potatoes, is all built of glucose. Chemists say that the very large starch molecule is made up of many smaller glucose molecules tied together.

Starch can be split in many ways, and it always finally gives glucose. That is what happens when starch is digested. The glucose then gets into the blood and is burned. Some of the glucose which is not burned gets into the liver, and there it builds "glycogen," which is also made of very large molecules and is very similar to plant starch.

Glucose is stored up in the animal body in the form of glycogen and is digested again when the body is starved.

Glucose is made from vegetable starches of all kinds. The chemical change through which starch is changed is called "hydrolysis." This word means dissolution with water. It can be done by heating with a dilute acid or with the help of natural enzymes.

Nearly all of the glucose so produced is directly changed into alcohol with other enzymes. Alcohol, which is necessary for many industries, is the goal of the process.

Glucose itself is not used very much. It is found chiefly in pastries and candy since it is cheaper than cane sugar. It comes mixed with water as a thick syrup. Glucose is also less sweet than cane sugar.

A language is not a lot of "rules and grammar." A language is the means by which one person expresses his thoughts and feelings to another person so that he understands them!

WHAT IS LANGUAGE?

A language could be made up of signs, or sounds, or facial expressions, or just gestures or bodily actions! Or it can be a combination of these things. When you have something to say you not only speak, you make gestures and facial expressions.

The test of whether we have a language is whether we are understood. If you invented a language of your own and nobody understood you, you would not have a true language.

As civilizations developed, people began to live in large groups, life became more complicated, more and more knowledge was acquired, and languages became more complicated and highly developed.

But surprisingly enough, we do not really know how languages began. Some think they began from the natural cries and exclamations that people made to express surprise, pleasure, or pain. Others think languages began by imitation of the sounds of nature. Still others believe that it began by imitating the sounds of animals. And it is possible that each of these methods had a part in the beginning of language, but how much we do not know.

We do know that practically all the languages spoken on earth today can be traced back to some common source; that is, an ancestor language which has many descendants. The ancestor language together with all the language which developed from it, is called a "family" of languages.

English is a member of the Indo-European family of languages. Other members of this family are French, Italian, German, Norwegian, and Greek.

INDEX

205

wrestling in, 170
Jardin des Plantes, 136
Jellyfish, 96–97
Jennet, 83
Jews:
  capital punishment among, 65
  graves of, 166
  music of, 139
  religion of, 156–57
Judicial duel, 137–38
Julian Calendar, 199
Juries, 157–58

K

Kale, 47
Kangaroos, 84

L

Languages:
  chimpanzee, 81
  English, 204
  Indo-European, 204
Lao-tse, 157
Lava, 27
Leather, tanning of, 9
Leaves:
  transpiration in, 10
  uses for man of, 67
Leprechauns, 52
Liberty Bell, 161–62
Lichens, Antarctic, 69
Licorice, 194
Life:
  in Antarctica, 69
  in Dead Sea, 46
  in desert, 77
  sun and, 31
  See also Evolution
Light, 174
  corpuscular theory of, 16
  of moon, 33
  spectrum of, 174
  speed of, 16
  of stars and planets, 30
  of sun, 30–31
  wave lengths and colors of, 15–16
Lightning, 37
Lions, *see* Cat family
Liquids:
  buoyancy and, 185–86
  osmosis and, 9–10
  surface tension of, 187
  See also Water
Lithography, 197–98
London, Tower of, 153
Lydians, 143
Lymph, 112

M

Magma, 27
Magnetism, 161
Magnetometer, 178

Mail, *see* Postal systems
Mammals:
  marsupial, 84–85
  reproduction in, 100, 101
Manatee, 100
Marsupials, 84–85
Mason and Dixon's Line, 53–54
Matches, 193
Matter, 17–18
Measurements, 174–75
Medicines and drugs, 9, 67, 194
Melons, 167–68
Metals:
  alchemy and, 195–96
  weights of, 58–59
Meteors and meteorites, 29–30
Micrometer, 175
Middle ages:
  alchemy in, 195–96
  capital punishment in, 65–66
  fire in, 193
  painting in, 142
  postal system in, 162–63
  umbrellas in, 160
  universities in, 155
Mile, 175
Milk, 21, 181–83
Milky Way, 72
Minerals:
  in Antarctica, 69
  in Dead Sea, 46
  in milk, 21
  in sand, 179
Mirrors, 190–91
Missing Link, 79
Missouri-Mississippi Rivers, 29
Mohammedanism, 156–57
Molecules, 17–18
  surface tension of, 187
Molting, 80
Money, 143
Monkeys, *see* Apes and monkeys
Monotheism, 157
Moon, 33–34
Morris, Robert, 147
Mosquitos, 86–87
Mosses, 7
  Antarctic, 69
Motion:
  centrifugal force and, 14–15
  of orbits, 173
  perpetual, 68
Mound Builders, 51
Mountains, tallest, 155
Mucus, 132
Muscles:
  cells of, 112
  exercise and, 123
Mushrooms, 14
Music, 139

N

Names of states, 145–46

Napkins, 170
Napoleonic eagle, 70
National emblems, 70–71
  See also Flags
Neanderthal man, 21–24
Neolithic Age, 23
Nerves, 126–27
  cells of, 112, 126–27
  speed of thought and, 133
New Year, 149
Newton, Sir Isaac, 14, 16, 173
Nicknames of states, 145–46
Nile River, 25, 48–49
North Magnetic Pole, 178
North Pole, 178
Northern Lights, 33
Northmen, *see* Vikings
Nose:
  mucus of, 132
  sense of smell and, 131–32
Nuclear fallout, 19–20

O

Oceans, 25, 28
Octopus, 97–98
Offset printing, 198
Old Stone Age, 22
Onions, 128
Opera, 139
Opossum, 84–85
Optical illusion, 128–29
Orbits, satellite, 173
Organic chemistry, 183–84
Osmosis, 9
Ozone, 33

P

Painting, 142
  cave, 21, 22
Paleobotany, 6
Papal States, 66–67
Paper, 196–97
Paris, University of, 155
Pasteurized milk, 182
Pathology, plant, 6
Pepper, 180
Periodic Table, 18
Perpetual motion, 68
Persians, postal system of, 162
Perspiration, 110
Petroleum, locating, 177–78
Philately, 40
Philosophers' stone, 196
Physical chemistry, 183–84
Physiological chemistry, 184
Physiology, plant, 6
Pigeons:
  homing, 95
  training of, 103
Pimples, 118–19
Pirates, 148–49
Pitcher plant, 86
Pituitary gland, 113
Pixies, 52
Planetarium, 171–72
Planets, 72

light from, 30
Plant lice, 107
Plants, 6–7
  Antarctic, 69
  chlorophyll in, 7
  desert, 77
  diseases of, 6, 62–63
  fallout and, 19–20
  fertilizers for, 201–2
  fossils of, 6
  insect-eating, 86
  non-green, 7, 111
  parasitic, 62
  poisonous, 10–11, 62
  pollination of, 13–14
  reproduction in, *see* Reproduction
  sap flow of, 9–10
Plastics, 181–82
Platinum, 58–59
Plimpton, J. J., 168
Poison, execution by, 65
Poison ivy, 10–11
Pollination, 13–14
Pompeii, 44–45
Pony Express, 163
Population census, 41–42
Postal systems, 162–63
Primates, 80–81
Printing:
  offset, 198
  presses and movable type, 141–42
Property, 194
Proteins, milk, 21
Protons, 17–18
Protoplasm, 7
Psychical research, 133–34
Ptolemy, 72–73
Purring, 83

Q

Qualitative and quantitative analysis, 183
Quicksand, 18–19
Quinine, 9

R

Radio, 33
Radioactive fallout, 19–20
Rain:
  clouds, 34–35
  rivers and, 28–29
  sleet as frozen, 38
Rainbows, 15–16
Rats, 90–91
Regent's Park, 136
Religions, 156–57
  monotheistic, 157
  of Vikings, 61
Reproduction:
  in mammals, 100
  in plants, 7, 13–14, 62–63
Reptiles, *see* Dinosaurs; Snakes
Resources, conservation of, 63–64